The

Ultimate

Office Survival

Guide

Leonard Rogoff, Ph.D.

 THOMSON ™
ARCO

Australia • Canada • Mexico • Singapore • Spain • United Kingdom • United States

An ARCO Book

ARCO is a registered trademark of Thomson Learning, Inc., and is used herein under license by Peterson's.

About The Thomson Corporation and Peterson's

With revenues of US$7.2 billion, The Thomson Corporation (www.thomson.com) is a leading global provider of integrated information solutions for business, education, and professional customers. Its Learning businesses and brands (www.thomsonlearning.com) serve the needs of individuals, learning institutions, and corporations with products and services for both traditional and distributed learning.

Peterson's, part of The Thomson Corporation, is one of the nation's most respected providers of lifelong learning online resources, software, reference guides, and books. The Education Supersite^{SM} at www.petersons.com—the internet's most heavily traveled education resources—has searchable databases and interactive tools for contacting U.S.-accredited institutions and programs. In addition, Peterson's serves more that 105 million education consumers annually.

For more information, contact Peterson's, 2000 Lenox Drive, Lawrenceville, NJ 08648; 800-338-3282; or find us on the World Wide Web at: www.petersons.com/about

ISBN 0-7689-1065-X

Printed in Canada

10 9 8 7 6 5 4 3 2 1   04 03 02

Contents

Introduction

The Ultimate Office Survival Guide offers models of standard business writing. Standard models are not inflexible, however, and writers should feel free to exercise personal judgment in adapting these examples to their own needs. Two basic rules: be consistent and use common sense.

Many business firms, especially large ones, employ their own house style. Other firms adhere to manuals published by various trade associations, newspapers, or university presses. Before starting on any business writing project, check to see if your company uses a particular style or guide book. You will want your work to reflect your company's policy.

This guide is organized to offer a handy, comprehensive program of the various types of business writing. Business Letter Basics offers an introduction to the elements of letter writing. Once you have mastered the skills of writing an introduction, body, and conclusion, you can apply these lessons to whatever situation is required. Sample Business Letters offers models. Your details may be unique, but the business letter follows a similar pattern. You will need to tailor the samples to your particular needs. Always remember that the purpose of a business letter is to win the reader's goodwill, so you might also think about what approach would be most convincing to you if you were receiving the letter. Keep in mind your intended audience.

Word processing and desktop publishing have opened new possibilities. Your company likely has preferences in its use of computer software and you will need to learn these systems. The company's correspondence may follow a standard format that is already programmed in the computer, or you may choose from a variety of types and designs. The basic rule of business writing is still to keep the page as clean and easy to read as possible.

With the rise of electronic communication via faxes and e-mails, you will need to learn your company's procedures. Note that faxes and e-mails do not have as many rules or conventions as do business letters. This guide offers some helpful models, but you will also have to use your common sense and good taste. This is true of minutes, which may be recorded on a computer notebook and sent as an attached file by e-mail. Again, you will need to take instructions from your company. Resumes, news releases, and business reports are usually sent by hard copy, that is, as paper documents. These practices, however, are changing.

The Ultimate Office Survival Guide also offers a basic introduction to the elements of grammar. The focus is on practical and common usage. You will need to have a fundamental familiarity with the terms of grammar to understand why certain choices are made. Good grammar reflects on the quality of your company, just as bad grammar raises questions about your capabilities. The sections on style and punctuation are also intended to offer basic troubleshooting skills.

The conclusion of the book contains reference sections on Forms of Address, Postal Abbreviations, and a Glossary of Basic Business Terms. It is important that you be familiar with the vocabulary used in the marketplace today, which changes rapidly.

Finally, as you do your business writing, remember that your letter, memo, or report conveys an image of your company to the outside world. Remember, too, it reflects your professional standards and competence.

Biography

Leonard Rogoff holds a Ph.D. in English from the University of North Carolina at Chapel Hill, where he served as director of the English Writing Laboratory. He has also served as Associate Professor of English at North Carolina Central University, a magazine staff writer, and an editor for several publishers. He has written widely for both popular and scholarly journals and is the author of *Homelands: Southern-Jewish Identity in Durham and Chapel Hill, North Carolina*. Sections on Grammar and Numbers are based on the work of Margaret A. Haller, M. A., author of *Office Guide to Business English*.

Chapter 1

Business Letter Basics

The business letter reflects the competence and professionalism of the person sending it. The quality of its contents and presentation is an advertisement for the company. Business letters should always be neat and easy to read. The format should be attractive and uncluttered. Always maintain a positive, courteous tone. The goal is to earn the goodwill of the person reading the letter.

Business letters will vary in format and content depending upon their purpose. The tone can be formal or informal, depending on the occasion. A business letter may be an invitation for a golfing date to a friend or an application for employment to a large, impersonal corporation. Be sure to strike an appropriate tone.

In a company or an organization, business letters usually follow a basic format. Check to see if your firm follows a particular manual or house style. Word-processing programs have defaults that will determine the width of margins, size and style of type fonts, ragged or justified (even) right margins, and so on. These defaults can be overridden, if necessary, to fit your company's house style.

Business letters can generally be divided into three parts that are as follows: A brief introductory paragraph states the reason for the letter and sets a courteous tone. Next, the body of the letter, consisting of one or more paragraphs, develops the major point with ample supporting detail. Lastly, the conclusion should be short, thanking the reader for their attention and suggesting possibilities for further action. If the message is very brief—a congratulatory note or confirmation of a meeting—then these points may be condensed into a paragraph or two.

Before sending the letter, be sure to proofread it carefully. If you are typing on a computer, be sure to check the spelling with the word-processing dictionary. Proofreading should be done slowly and letter-by-letter. Several readings are often necessary to catch all mistakes.

A model business letter is included here to give you a guide to the format of a business letter. To follow is a breakdown of the letter components and a description of their purpose and placement in a business letter. Note that each component has a corresponding number that matches its description.

Model Business Letter

```
                          COMPANY LETTERHEAD
1                            Street Address
                              City, State

                              (2-6 spaces)

2                                                    month day, year
                              (3-8 spaces)

   Addressee, Title
3  Street Address
                               (2 spaces)

4  ATTENTION: LINE
                               (3 spaces)

5  Dear Addressee:
                               (2 spaces)

6  Subject: Typing Instructions
                               (2 spaces)
```

7   The text of a business letter is single spaced with double spacing be-
    tween paragraphs.

8   The left and right margins should be set two inches for short letters,
    one and a half inches for medium-length letters, and one inch for long
    letters.

9   The bottom margin is at least one and a half inches or six lines.

```
                               (2 spaces)

                            Complimentary close,

10                     (4-6 spaces for signature)

                            Writer's name, Title

                               (2 spaces)
```

11 Initials

```
                              (1-2 spaces)
```

12 Enclosures

Parts of a Business Letter

Letterhead (1)

Businesses usually have letterhead stationery, which contains the company's logo, name, address, fax and telephone numbers, e-mail and Web site addresses, and other pertinent information. If the stationery is not letterhead, then type the writer's address in the upper right-hand corner:

Street
City, State ZIP

Do not use abbreviations for the street or city. The U.S. Postal Service's two-letter state abbreviations may be used. For more information, consult the Postal Service Abbreviations chapter.

Dateline (2)

The date is typed at least three lines below the letterhead either on the left margin or the right margin, depending on letter style. If the letter is brief, leave more spaces under the letterhead to give the letter a balanced appearance. If the stationery lacks a letterhead, type the date under the city and state of the writer's address.

Dates may follow several forms:

Traditional	month day, year
	May 27, 2002
Science, military, government	day month year
	27 May 2002
informal, handwritten letters	month/day/year
	5/27/02
informal (European style)	day/month/year
	27/5/02

Mail Notation

If the letter has been sent by express mail, special delivery, certified, or registered mail, then a notation may be printed in capitals on the left margin. It may appear at the top of the letter two lines below the date or at the bottom of the letter two lines below the final typed line. Mail notations often are typed only on copies.

(near the top of the letter)

4 Lake Lenore Road
Poeville, MD 00000
December 27, 2002

CERTIFIED MAIL
Ms. Angela Torres
26 Snowtown Boulevard
Edina, MN 00000

(near the bottom of the letter)

Yours truly,
Jennifer Jordan, President

JJ/hw
CERTIFIED MAIL

Confidential Notation

If the letter is to be read only by the addressee, then type PERSONAL or CONFIDENTIAL in capitals on the left margin and four lines under the date. If a mail notation appears at the top, type the personal or confidential notation directly under it.

Inside Address (3)

The inside address, typed flush on the left margin, contains information about the person or company that receives the letter. It should conform to the address on the envelope. Usually, it consists of the following three parts:

Person or company
Street address
City, State ZIP

Use *Mr., Mrs., Ms.,* or *Dr.* before the person's name and, if it is short, the person's position in the company:

> Mr. Alex Kilgore, Manager
>
> Ms. Tanya Simmons, Supervisor

If the title is long, then it may be placed under the name:

> Mr. Alex Kilgore
> District Sales Manager
>
> Ms. Tanya Simmons
>
> Human Relations Supervisor

For ministers, medical doctors, and other professionals who hold doctoral degrees, use either *Dr.* or *Doctor* before the name, or put the degree after the name:

> Michelle Joseph, Ph.D.
>
> *or*
>
> Doctor Michelle Joseph
>
> Reverend Thomas Leach, D.D.
>
> *or*
>
> Reverend Dr. Thomas Leach

The same principle holds true for lawyers who use *Esquire*:

> Mr. John Curry
>
> *or*
>
> John Curry, Esq.

Print the name of the company as it appears on the company's letterhead:

> Angelo Bros. Candles
>
> Smith & Guthridge
>
> D. Mills Inc.
>
> Ex/Ron Corporation

Avoid using abbreviations in the street, city, and state address except for official U.S. Postal Service codes:

Mr. Charles Huang, President
Home Office Systems
34 Stratford Court
Del Mar, CA 00000

Mr. Robert Kowalski
Vice President of Operations
Castro Steel, Incorporated
2 Industrial Parkway
Gary, IN 00000

Attention Line (4)

An attention line is frequently included in business letters that are addressed impersonally to a company. Such a letter is intended for a specific person, position, or division. Several styles are acceptable:

Attention: Mr. Malik Lipscomb

Attention: Mr. Malik Lipscomb, Sales Manager

Attention: Sales Manager

ATTENTION Sales Division

ATTENTION—Malik Lipscomb

The attention line should appear two lines beneath the inside address. When using an attention line, omit the person's name from the inside address. Use an impersonal greeting—not the name on the attention line:

Drexler Electric Company

117 East Eighteenth Street

New York, NY 00000

Attention: Parts Manager

Sir or Madam:

Salutation (5)

The salutation is the greeting to the reader of the letter. Use the name and title of the person listed in the inside address.

Dr. Gerald Royster
23 Charlotte Road
Topeka, KS 00000

Dear Dr. Royster,

Salutations establish a relationship between the reader and the writer, which can be either formal or informal. If you know the reader well and desire a casual tone, use an informal salutation. Official business correspondence usually requires a formal greeting although the current trend is to be more informal. To be very formal, omit the personal *dear*.

Very formal	Formal	Informal
Sir:	Dear Dr. Royster,	Dear Jerry,
Madam:	Dear Ms. Johnson,	Dear Tony,
Sir or Madam:	Dear Prof. Schwartz,	Dear Vitaly,
Staff:	Dear Marketing Associates,	Everyone,

Use either the first name or the last name of the addressee in a salutation, not both. If you do not know whether a woman is married or not, use Ms. If you are unsure whether the person is a man or a woman, then you may use first and last names:

Dear Lee Jones:

Dear Brooks Smith:

If you do not know who will be reading the letter, then use a salutation that includes all possible readers. For this reason, use a greeting that does not define the reader's gender:

Dear Sir or Madam:

Dear Madam or Sir:

Dear Friend:

Dear Customer:

Dear Staff:

In standard punctuation, a colon is placed after the salutation in a business letter. A comma is used only in a personal letter. Some businesses use an open punctuation style that does not require a punctuation mark after the salutation. Check the house style preferred by your business.

Subject Line (6)

A subject line informs the reader briefly about the letter's contents. Many styles are acceptable, including the ones that follow:

Subject: Computer sales

SUBJECT: Inventory Control

Subject—Revised Pricing Policy

Subject: New Credit Guidelines

Subject: Order No. 7176X

CONTRACT NEGOTIATIONS

Some companies prefer to use the Latin word *re* (thing) in place of *subject*:

Re: Computer sales

RE: Inventory Control

The subject line is located two spaces directly under the salutation:

Dear Mr. Lee:

Subject: Computer sales

Dear Ms. Hernandez,

CONTRACT NEGOTIATIONS

Introduction (7)

The opening of a business letter should state the writer's purpose and set the tone for the letter. It should capture the reader's attention and establish a link between writer and reader. The opening should also be brief. Two or three lines are sufficient.

Macrovision is pleased to announce that the Sportstime channel is now as part of its Ultraservice plan. We invite you to upgrade your standard package to take advantage of the unique programming available on America's premier sports network.

Body (8)

The body of a business letter contains one or more paragraphs that provide detailed supporting facts or further explanation. These points should be developed logically, step by step, and as clearly as possible. Include all the necessary information—but no more—and maintain a positive tone.

With Ultraservice you will enjoy a complete package of family television. In addition to all the channels included in the standard package, Ultraservice includes such popular features as the Toons children's channel, Global Education Network, and now Sportstime. You will enjoy a broad array of some of the best sports programming available on television, including coverage of the ABC Conference, one of America's most competitive collegiate leagues. Sportstime also has exclusive coverage of minor-league baseball and basketball where you can see the stars of tomorrow.

Conclusion (9)

The final paragraph of a business letter should end on a positive note; it should encourage the reader to respond favorably to the message of the letter. If possible, conclude with a personal remark, suggesting an appointment or expressing a desire for more communication.

Ultraservice can be yours with only a phone call today. Macrovision will be pleased to give you the upgraded service free for thirty days. If not satisfied, you may cancel at any time. Call Macrovision today for the best in television.

Complimentary Close (10)

As does the salutation, the complimentary close reflects the relationship between writer and reader. Thus, the close should maintain the same tone as the salutation. If the salutation uses the reader's first name, then choose an informal complimentary close and sign with the reader's first name, even if first and last names are typed. If you address the reader by the last name, then a more formal complimentary close is usually appropriate.

Very formal	*Formal*
Respectfully,	Yours truly,
Respectfully yours,	Yours very truly,
	Very truly yours,

Informal	*Very informal*
Sincerely,	Best,
Sincerely yours,	Best wishes,
Cordially,	Regards,
Cordially yours,	

Only the first word in a complimentary close is capitalized. A comma follows the last word. The writer's name should be typed under the complimentary close, leaving three to five spaces for the signature:

Yours truly,   Cordially yours,

Emily Pratt   Frank Chan
Emily Pratt   Frank Chan

The title of the writer may be added after the name—if the title is short. Separate the name and title by a comma or a hyphen:

Ginna Curry, Director

You may also list the writer's title after the name and then type the division or department under it:

Sal Mazza, Chairman
Department of Engineering

To emphasize that the company rather than the signer is responsible for the letter, the company's name may appear two lines under the complimentary close. The writer's name is typed four lines beneath that:

Yours truly,
Plaza Associates
Joseph Hassan, President

Identification Initials (11)

Identification or reference initials indicate who wrote, dictated, and typed the letter. Usually, the writer's initials are typed in capitals followed by the secretary's initials. The identification initials are typed on the left margin two lines beneath the signature block. Several styles are acceptable:

LBR/as   LBR:as
LBR/AS   LBR:AS

Enclosures (12)

If other materials are included with the letter, then add an enclosure notation on the left margin two lines below the identification initials or the signature block. The notation may be written out or abbreviated:

Enclosure
Enc.
Encl.

If you itemize the enclosures, then a colon or dash may be added:

Enclosure: application form
                brochure
Enclosure—application form, brochure

After the enclosure note, you may list the number of items that are included:

Encl. 2
Enclosures—2
Enclosures (2)
Enc.2

If you include more than one enclosure of if the enclosures are important, then list them by name:

Enclosures:	Encl.
Copyright Form	Check
Letter of Credit	Catalogue
Contract	Order Form

To follow are some other components you can use for your business letters.

Copies

If copies are sent to other persons, a copy notation is added two lines below the identification initials or enclosure notation, whichever is last. CC stands for carbon copy. Several styles are acceptable:

cc
cc:
CC
CC:
Copies to

You may list the initials, names, or names and addresses of those who receive copies:

cc   Dr. Jacob Pasternack
      Mr. Gus Spelman
      Ms. Haley Saunders

cc: JP
     GS
     HS

Copy to Dr. Jacob Pasternack
      213 Knightsbridge Way
      Columbia, MD 00000

If you do not want the reader of the letter to know that copies are being sent, then use a notation for blind carbon copy on the copies only:

bcc
bcc:
BCC
BCC:

Postscripts

In business letters, a postscript is used only to emphasize an important point, not to include information that was left out of the letter. In sales letters, a postscript may highlight a final selling point. Postscripts are single-spaced two lines below the last notation. Use one of the following abbreviations:

P.S.
PS.
PS:
PS—

For example:

P.S. If you order within ten days, I am authorized to offer a 10 percent discount.

Multipage Letter

If possible, try to fit the contents of your letter onto one page; a one-page letter is easier to read and to handle than a multipage letter. If the second page is only three or four lines long, then try to include the information on the first page. With the possible exception of sales letters, especially unsolicited advertising, do not use the back of the page.

Do not use letterhead stationery for additional pages, but use paper of the same quality as the first page. Six spaces from the top of the second page, starting on the left-hand margin, type a heading to identify the letter:

Fazio Motors   -2-   August 19, 2002

Fazio Motors
Page 2
August 19, 2002

Fazio Motors
2
August 19, 2002

The text begins four lines below the heading.

Paper

Business letters should be written on high-quality paper. Banks and law offices usually specify 100 percent rag paper. A bond paper with a watermark is suitable for business use. For most business letters, choose a 20-pound weight, white bond paper. Twenty-four pound weight may used for important letters. For copies and overseas airmail, 6- to 13-pound weight is sufficient. These papers are known as tissue or onionskin.

Use	Size
General business correspondence	$8\frac{1}{2}$" $\times$ 11" or
	$8\frac{1}{2}$" $\times$ $10\frac{1}{2}$"
Executive stationery	$7\frac{1}{2}$" $\times$ $10\frac{1}{2}$"
Notes and memos	$5\frac{1}{2}$" $\times$ $10\frac{1}{2}$"

Typing Instructions

Spacing

Except for very short letters, business letters should be single-spaced with double-spaces between paragraphs. Very short letters of fifty words or less may be double-spaced, including addresses, with triple spacing between paragraphs. Half-sheet paper $5\frac{1}{2}$" $\times$ $8\frac{1}{2}$" may be used for short letters. A business letter should appear attractive and orderly. In order to balance the text on the page, the number of spaces between the letterhead, date, and inside address may vary from two to six spaces.

Margins

The size of the margins is dictated by the length of the letter. Try to balance the text in the center of the page.

Short letters	2-inch margins
Medium-length letters	1-inch margins
Long letters	1-inch margins

Margins may be ragged or justified. A ragged margin will be aligned on the left margin, but not on the right margin:

> The typist must choose how to set the margins. Ragged margins will leave more blank space on the page, often making it easier to read. The word-processing program may be set to default with a ragged margin.

A justified margin will be evenly aligned on the right as well as on the left:

> With the use of word processors many typists prefer to justify the margins. It creates a neater balanced look, especially with block style. Word-processing programs will wrap the text so that the right margin will be evenly aligned. This style is commonly used now.

Check, once again, to see if your company has a preference for ragged or justified margins.

Letter Formats

Several formats are acceptable in typing the business letter: block, modified block, modified semi-block, simplified, and indented. The trend today is toward simpler, less cluttered styles, using minimal punctuation. Check to see the style that your company prefers.

Standard Punctuation

Standard or mixed punctuation is the most popular style. It is used with block, modified block, or semi-block styles. The salutation ends with a colon, and the complimentary close is followed by a comma. The dateline and addresses include interior punctuation, but no end punctuation is used.

June 6, 2002

Mr. Jose Pagano
Sterling Mortgage Company
16 Williams Court
Albuquerque, NM 00000

Dear Mr. Pagano:

Open Punctuation

Open punctuation is required for letters in simplified style and optional for block style. Salutations and complimentary closes may be eliminated, but if used, no punctuation follows. The comma is retained between the day and year in the dateline and between the city and state in addresses, but no punctuation appears at the end of the lines.

June 6, 2002

Mr. Jose Pagano
Sterling Mortgage Company
16 Williams Court
Albuquerque, NM 00000

Dear Mr. Pagano

Closed Punctuation

Closed punctuation is used mostly with the indented letter style. This style is not used in the United States, but is still employed in Europe. Commas are placed at the end of each line in the address—except for the last, which ends with a period. A period also follows the dateline. The salutation is followed by a colon, and commas are placed at the end of each line of the complimentary close, signature block, and notations. A period is placed at the end of the signature block and notations.

Sample Letter Formats

Block Style

<pre>
                    COMPANY LETTERHEAD
                      Street Address
                      City, State ZIP

Month day, year

Addressee, Title
Company
Street Address
City, State ZIP

ATTENTION NAME

Dear Addressee

The block style is easy to read. The date, inside address, salutation,
paragraphs, and signature are all typed flush on the left margin.

The block letter may use open or standard (mixed) punctuation. This
letter uses the open pattern. Note that no punctuation follows the saluta-
tion or the complimentary close. For ease of reading, all punctuation is
kept to a minimum. Since this is a letter of medium length, the margins are
one and a half inches on all sides. Extra blank lines are left between the
dateline, inside address, and attention line to center the text on the page.
The number of blank lines may vary between two to six lines depending on
the length of the letter.

This letter also contains a complimentary close two lines under the final
line of text. At least four lines are left for the signature. The
secretary's initials and other end notes follow two lines below the
signature block.

Complimentary close,

Signature

Signer's Name

Title

Ini

Enclosure
</pre>

Modified Block Style

COMPANY LETTERHEAD
Street Address
City, State ZIP

Month day, year

Addressee
Title
Company
Street Address
City, State ZIP

Dear Addressee:

The modified block style is a variation of block style. The chief difference is that the date is typed flush on the right margin, and the complimentary close and signature block are also aligned on the right side of the page. The inside address, salutation, paragraph blocks, and end notation are typed flush on the left margin.

The modified block letter uses mixed punctuation. Thus, a colon appears at the end of the addressee's names in the salutation, and a comma is used after the complimentary close.

Spacing is also designed to give the letter a balanced look on the page. The secretary's initials appear two lines under the signature, followed by an enclosure note.

Complimentary close,

Signature

Signer's Name, Title

Ini

Enclosure

Simplified Style

COMPANY LETTERHEAD
Street Address
City, State ZIP

Month day year

Addressee
Title
Company
Street Address
City State ZIP

SUBJECT LINE

The simplified letter is another variation of block form. It was devised by the Administrative Management Society to simplify work for secretaries and to save time for readers. It uses open punctuation.

The simplified letter is typed in block format: dateline, inside address, paragraphs, signature block, and end notations are all typed flush on the left margin. A salutation and complimentary close are eliminated, and a subject line in capitals is substituted for the salutation. Three blank lines separate the subject line from both the inside address and opening paragraph.

This letter is centered on the page. Since it is of medium length, three blank lines are left between the letterhead and dateline. The same space was left above the inside address. The signer's name and title appear in capitals. End notes follow block style form.

Signature

SIGNER'S NAME, TITLE

ini

Encl.

Modified Semi-Block Style

```
                    COMPANY LETTERHEAD
                    Street Address
                    City, State ZIP

                                           Month day, year

     Addressee
     Title
     Company
     Street Address
     City, State ZIP

     Dear Addressee:

        The modified semi-block letter is also an acceptable form. Like the
     modified block letter, it places the date and complimentary close on the
     right margin near the center of the page. The inside address, salutation,
     paragraph blocks, and end notations appear on the left margin.

        Note that the opening line of each paragraph is indented five to ten
     spaces. Standard or mixed punctuation is most often used in this form.
     This letter is of moderate length and the margins are set at one and a half
     inches. The complimentary close follows two lines after the final para-
     graph and the secretary's initials are two lines beneath that.

        The secretary should check to see the exact style preferred by the
     company before adapting this or any style.

                                           Complimentary close,

                                           Signature

                                           Signer's Name

                                           Title


     ini

     Enclosures
```

Indented Style

```
                          COMPANY LETTERHEAD
                            Street Address
                            City, State ZIP


                                                   Month day, year

        Addressee,
           Company,
              Street,
                 City, Country


        Dear Addressee:

           The indented letter is not used in the United States, but it is still
        employed in Europe. The date appears on the right margin or near the
        center of the page. The first line of the inside address is flush on the left
        margin, but each subsequent lie is indented five spaces. The first line of
        each paragraph is indented five to ten spaces.

           The indented letter uses closed punctuation. Commas follow each line of
        the inside address, signature block, and end notations except the last
        line, which ends with a period. No punctuation follows the secretary's
        initials.

           Again, this format does not appear in the United States, but it may be
        seen in foreign correspondence.


                                           Complimentary close,

                                           Signature

                                           Signer's Name,

                                           Title


        ini

        cc
```

Sample Business Letters

Acknowledgment Letter

A letter of acknowledgment confirms a business transaction and indicates that your company is acting on it.

Purpose

1. To respond to an order

2. To advise of a shipment date or a service call

3. To thank a customer for a purchase, payment, or inquiry

Form

Introduction

- refer specifically to the customer's request

- thank customer for interest

Body

- mention order number

- describe in detail the product or service

- include time and means of delivery

Conclusion

- expression appreciation for business

- encourage further transactions

Burlage Furniture Company
23 Arroyo Road
San Diego, CA 00000
Phone: 000.III.2222
Fax: 000.III.2222

Mr. Abed Darwish
Purchasing Agent
Williams & Manuel, Inc.
7671 Doherty Drive
El Cajon CA 00000

Dear Mr. Darwish:

We appreciate your purchase of Trendmaster Office Furniture from Burlage.
We are sure that it will give your company many years of dependable and
satisfactory use.

Delivery is scheduled by California Freight for the morning of June 9. Your
order (Invoice #B11654) includes three Model A32 Trendmaster Computer
Desks with three Model C#@ Comfortback Chairs. As you requested, the desks
have a walnut finish, and the chairs are upholstered in tan naugehyde.
Please inspect all merchandise upon delivery, as Burlage Furniture cannot
be responsible for damage in shipping. All Burlage merchandise carries a
one-year warranty against defects in design or manufacture.

Once again, we appreciate your confidence in our product. We invite you to
visit our online catalog at http://www.BurlageFurniture.com for your office needs.

Sincerely,

Brian Boone

Sales Manager

ES/lbr

Enclosures

Application Letter

An application letter introduces the writer to a potential employer.

Purpose

1. To promote your qualifications for the job

2. To document your education and work experience

3. To arrange an interview

4. To persuade the reader to hire you

Form

Introduction

▩ announce your intention to apply for the position

▩ state where you heard about the opening

Body

▩ document your qualifications

▩ list your relevant work and educational experience in logical order

Conclusion

▩ state your willingness to be interviewed

▩ thank the reader for considering your application

▩ refer to resume or recommendations

73 Elm Street
Manassas, VA 00000

February 7, 2002

Ms. Francine Paliouras
Leesburg Real Estate
1406 Jones Street
Leesburg, Virginia 00000

Dear Ms. Paliouras:

I wish to apply for the position of receptionist and secretary that
Leesburg Real Estate advertised in the *Leesburg Dispatch* on February 3.
Having worked many years in a real-estate office, I feel confident that my
qualifications meet your needs.

My education and work experience have given me excellent secretarial
skills. After graduating from Stonewall Jackson High School in 1996, I
enrolled in Lynch County Community College, where I received an associate degree in secretarial science. I have mastered several word-processing programs and am familiar with most spreadsheet packages. Since 1998,
I have worked as a secretary and receptionist at Bull Run Realty. I have
responsibility for all business correspondence from our office, including
real-estate contracts.

I would be glad to meet with you for an interview. I can be reached at home
after 5:00 on weekdays or all day on weekends; my phone number is 000-
1111. Enclosed is my résumé including references. I look forward to
hearing from you.

Sincerely,

Keisha Powell

Follow-up Letter (job application)

This letter acquaints a prospective employer with your persistent interest in an advertised position. The follow-up letter can be strategically sent at any stage of the application process, particularly if your application has not been acknowledged. It may also be sent after an interview. Such a letter should link you to previous communications with the potential employer.

Purpose

1. To remind the reader of your recent exchange

2. To reiterate your interest in the position

3. To keep your identity alive in the reader's mind

Form

Introduction

▦ state date and nature of prior exchange

Body

▦ comment on continued interest in the position

▦ state your suitability for the position

Conclusion

▦ request permission to keep in touch

▦ express hope of a response

73 Elm Street
Manassas, VA 00000

March 1, 2002

Ms. Francine Paliouras
Leesburg Real Estate
1406 Jones Street
Leesburg, VA 00000

Dear Ms. Paliouras:

I sent you my resume and letter of application in answer to your advertisement for a receptionist and secretary in the February 3 *Leesburg
Dispatch.*

Having worked for sixteen years in residential real estate, I have the
skills and experience to benefit Leesburg Real Estate. My present position is in a firm that is closing its home sales division. I enjoy meeting
potential home buyers and would like to continue working with a firm that
specializes in residential properties. I know that Leesburg Real Estate
has been a regional leader in this field.

I would very much appreciate learning if my application has reached you.
I would be glad to submit further information about my qualifications. I
may be reached at the above address, or feel free to call me at 000-1111.

Sincerely,

Keisha Powell

Appointment Letter

An appointment letter details plans for a meeting or conference. For important engagements especially, a letter will verify the time, place, date, and purpose of the meeting.

Purpose

1. To specify time and location of a meeting

2. To confirm the appointment

Form

Introduction

▩ detail date, time, and place

Body

▩ review reasons for the meeting

▩ discuss any preparations

Conclusion

▩ express pleasure about meeting

KIEBER INVESTMENT ASSOCIATES
111 EAST NINTH STREET, SUITE 23
NEW YORK, NY 00000
www.Kia.net
000.111.2222

May 14, 2002

Mr. Chuang Chiu
Design Consultant
ASR Interiors
43 Madison Avenue
New York, NY 00000

Dear Chuang:

I want to confirm our appointment for lunch at Chez Alex on Tuesday, May 27, at 12:30.

I have reviewed your preliminary drawings for our new offices, and they look well designed. You handled the enlarged reception area very well. Would it be possible for you to bring to the meeting an extra set of blueprints to pass along to our partners?

I look forward to the meeting. I believe we can resolve the few remaining problems then.

Best wishes,

Joseph Kilgore

JK/bce

Appreciation Letter

A letter of appreciation is a personal way to thank a person or a company for extraordinary help or cooperation, especially for a donation to charity. Such a letter may be sent to customers to thank them for their business. A letter of appreciation may consist of a one- or two-paragraph note.

Purpose

1. To encourage further efforts

2. To acknowledge assistance

3. To express thanks

Form

Introduction

- state thanks

- set cordial tone

Body

- detail services or benefits available

- offer support to the reader

Conclusion

- express confidence

- seek to motivate the reader

Phillips Foundation
17 Schoolhouse Road
Lima, Ohio 00000
E-mail: Phillips@internet.com
Phone: 000.111.2222
Fax: 000.111.2222

December 27, 2002

Ms. Jill Swanson
Willett Editorial Associates
33 Moby Road
Sandusky, Ohio 00000

Dear Ms. Swanson:

On behalf of the Phillips Foundation, I thank you and your staff for the extraordinary help in preparing our annual report. Your efforts are greatly appreciated.

The report looks splendid and has received much praise from our board. We apologize again for delivering the manuscript to you later than promised. Your staff performed beyond the call of duty in meeting the publication deadline for our annual meeting. Far from looking like a rush job, the report is very professional.

I just want you to know that the Phillips Foundation appreciates your efforts and we look forward to many years of continued business.

Sincerely,

Ian Joseph

President

tb

Collection Letter (first request)

The collection letter requests payment of money owed. The tone of a first request should be firm and persuasive, but friendly, to ensure the customer's cooperation and continued business.

Purpose

1. To receive payment as quickly as possible

2. To maintain the customer's goodwill

Form

Introduction

■ state desire for payment

Body

■ describe in detail the nature of the debt

■ review previous notices of payment

■ suggest means of payment

Conclusion

■ thank reader for action on payment

■ promote goodwill

ROYAL LUMBER COMPANY
455 Schuyler Avenue
Kearny, NJ 00000
Phone: 000.111.2222   Fax: 000.111.2222

November 19, 2002

Mr. Joshua Jonathan
Lake Lenore Construction
18 Maurice Boulevard
Denville, New Jersey 00000

Dear Mr. Jonathan:

We remind you that payment of your account at Roval Lumber is past due.

According to our records your account shows an outstanding debt of $484.32 for a casement window that was delivered on October 3 (Invoice #8364; your purchase order #7B88). We mailed you a collection notice on November 1, but have not yet received your payment. If you are not able to pay the balance in full at this time, please let us know and we will arrange an installment plan with you.

We greatly appreciate your immediate attention to this matter and anticipate hearing from you soon. Please disregard this notice if your check is in the mail.

Cordially,

Helen Howard

Comptroller

Enclosures

1. Invoice #8364 (copy)

2. Credit statement

Collection Letter (subsequent requests)

If an account is long overdue and reminders, either by letter or phone, have failed to secure payment, subsequent collection letters should be increasingly stronger and more demanding in tone. The letter may warn about possible legal action, repossession, the intervention of a collection agency, loss of credit rating, or garnisheeing of wages (where permitted). The letter may also note that the company is taking these actions reluctantly, having been forced to act by the customer's failure to fulfill his or her obligation.

Purpose

1. To demand immediate payment

2. To warn customer of negative consequences

Form

Introduction

■ state strongly the need for immediate payment

■ emphasize creditor's responsibility

Body

■ state amount of debt

■ review history of collection efforts

Conclusion

■ warn of negative consequences of inaction

■ demand immediate payment

ROVAL LUMBER COMPANY
455 Schuyler Avenue
Kearny, NJ 00000
Phone: 000.111.2222   Fax: 000.111.2222

December 15, 2002

Mr. Joshua Jonathan
Lake Lenore Construction
18 Maurice Boulevard
Denville, New Jersey 00000

Dear Mr. Jonathan:

Your account at Roval Lumber is two months past due. If payment is not received immediately, we will have to take appropriate action.

Our records show an unpaid balance of $484.32. An installment payment was requested on November 19. Two notices have been sent since then. A minimum payment of $100 within five days will maintain your credit. We refer all our delinquent accounts to the Merchant's Credit Bureau.

We can continue to offer credit only if our customers meet their obligations. Please send your payment at once. Otherwise, Roval Lumber will have no choice but to turn over your account to the collection agency.

Sincerely,

Helen Howard, Comptroller

Collection Letter (first notice, preprinted)

This form letter serves as a first notice of a payment due. Blanks are left for the date, inside address, salutation, and such relevant data as the sum owed and the deadline. You may have a formatted notice in your computer program or you may use preprinted forms.

Purpose

1. To attract attention

2. To elicit payment of a past due account

Form

Introduction

▓ note the sum due

Body

▓ request payment

Conclusion

▓ express thanks for the payment

CARPET UNIVERSE

811 San Pedro Road

Armadillo, Texas 00000

(000) 000-0000

_____
(date)

_____

_____

_____
(inside address)

Dear _____:
(addressee)

Our credit department reports that your balance of   (amount)   is past
due on   (date).

We greatly appreciate your prompt payment of this sum. Thank you for
your attention to this matter.

Sincerely,

_____
Credit Manager

Collection Letter (follow up, preprinted)

The collection letter may use a preprinted form. The letter may consist of a preprinted card enclosed in an envelope with a copy of the bill. You may format the collection letter as a file in your word-processing program and tailor it to the individual customer.

Purpose

1. To attract attention

2. To elicit payment of an account past due

Form

Introduction

■ name creditor

Body

■ state sum and date due

Conclusion

■ list name of account, balance, and current date

CAROL ARTHUR FASHION

23 Jordan Street
Chicago, IL 00000
000.111.2222

Dear Customer:

Your balance is past due as of _____. We would appreciate imme-
diate payment.
Account name: _____
Amount due: _____
Date: _____

CAROL ARTHUR FASHION

23 Jordan Street
Chicago, IL 00000
000.111.2222

Dear Customer:

Your balance remains past due since _____, so we must again urge
you to remit payment immediately.
Account name: _____
Amount due: _____
Date: _____

CAROL ARTHUR FASHION

23 Jordan Street
Chicago, IL 00000
000.111.2222

Dear Customer:

We urgently request that you immediately pay your balance of
_____, which has been outstanding since _____ despite
multiple notices from us.
Account name: _____
Amount due: _____
Date: _____

Complaint Letter

The complaint letter expresses dissatisfaction with a service or a product. Although the problem may arouse anger, a complaint letter should be firm, precise, and controlled in tone. The writer wants to persuade the reader to respond favorably by correcting the problem or by making an adjustment.

Purpose

1. To inform the reader of an unsatisfactory service or product

2. To receive compensation for the problem

Form

Introduction

▓ identify the problem

▓ state reason for the complaint

Body

▓ give details about the product or service

▓ explain how you were inconvenienced

▓ request correction, compensation, or adjustment

Conclusion

▓ politely but firmly express thanks for action

▓ encourage goodwill

Leonard Enterprises/111 Duncan Drive, San Antonio TX 00000
www.Leonard.org
000.111.2222

A-Rog Hair Products
12 Chauve Street
Chapel Hill NC 00000

Dear Sir or Madam:

On May 27, 2001, I purchased a one-year supply of A-Rog Hair Enchancer at Weiner Drugs. Included in the package was a guarantee that promised "complete customer satisfaction in six months or your money back." After six months of using your product without any increased hair growth, I am requesting a refund.

I do not feel that A-Rog Hair Enchancer lived up to the promise of its claims. I followed the directions in the instruction booklet by taking the medication daily and applying the topical treatment weekly. Your claim that A-Rog provides a "cure for all forms of hair loss" including "male-pattern baldness" was not verified by my experience. Furthermore, I suffered some negative side effects including indigestion.

Please refund my purchase price of $149.95. Enclosed is a box top with bar code and a copy of my cash-register receipt. I purchased your product in good faith and have every expectation that A-Rog will stand by its guarantee. For many years I have used A-Rog shampoo and conditioner and would like to remain a loyal customer of your brand.

Sincerely,

Leonard Sanscheveu

Enc: bar code

receipt

Congratulatory Letter

Congratulations are sent to a business contact to recognize promotions, awards, or special achievements. A letter of congratulations may be a one- or two-paragraph note and can be handwritten if you wish to be very personal.

Purpose

1. To express admiration

2. To motivate through praise

3. To promote goodwill

Form

Introduction

■ state achievement

■ set congratulatory tone

Body

■ remark on appropriateness of recognition

Conclusion

■ express personal pride in the accomplishment

CUTTER CREATIVE MANAGEMENT
SUITE 1501, TBA PLAZA
BOSTON, MA 00000
WWW.CUTTERCREATIVE.ORG
000.111.2222

April 23, 2002

Valeria Ebed
CDK Advertising
16 Charles Street
Boston, MA 00000

Dear Val:

I was delighted to read in *Advertising Today* that you've been awarded the

Edgecomb Foundation's Silver Quill Prize for ad copy. I've always thought

that your work was the best in the industry and I'm glad to see you get the

recognition that you deserve.

Best,

Doug Hecht

acb

Credit Denied Letter

A letter denying a request for credit preserves goodwill by maintaining a positive tone. It should be frank but tactful. Do not begin with the explicit refusal of credit, but suggest means to continue the customer's business.

Purpose

1. To inform the customer that purchases can only be made on a cash basis

2. To encourage the customer to continue business and improve credit rating

Form

Introduction

■ review circumstances of credit request

■ express thanks for customer's interest

Body

■ state company policy on granting credit

■ express regret at customer's current financial status

Conclusion

■ suggest alternatives to credit buying

■ invite further correspondence

PROCOM BUSINESS COMPUTERS/ 12 ELM STREET/ PHOENIX, AZ 00000
WWW.PROCOM.NET procom@internet.net 000.111.2222

August 19, 2002

Ms. Elizabeth Perski
Sunburst Organic Grocers
21 Attermeier Drive
Tucson, AZ 00000

Dear Ms. Perski:

We are grateful for the promptness with which you supplied the financial
statement that we requested to open a credit line. Your determination to
expand a small business in the current economic climate is commendable. We
appreciate your interest in the Databank cash register, the best product on
the market for small businesses.

Our first step in considering applications for credit is to examine the
applicant's bottom line for profitability after twenty-four consecutive
months of business. As your venture is but six months old, we regret that we
cannot at this time extend a line of credit.

We will be glad to do business with you on a cash basis for now, and will
review your credit standing at the appropriate time. If your capitaliza-
tion changes, please let us know. We wish you luck with your enterprise and
hope that we can be of future service to you.

Sincerely,

Jackson Knifechief,

Credit Manager

JK/as

Credit Granted Letter

A letter granting credit should be affirmative, encouraging the customer to make purchases. The letter should clearly state the credit limit and the billing procedures in detail. If the credit request accompanies an order, then make note of its shipment.

Purpose

1. To notify applicant of a line of credit

2. To define the credit limit

3. To describe purchase and billing procedures

Form

Introduction

- express pleasure at applicant's financial status

- state line of credit granted

- note shipment of purchased goods (optional)

Body

- detail the credit arrangement

- comment on benefits and limitations

Conclusion

- express optimism over ongoing relationship

- invite more business

GOTHIC STAINED GLASS SUPPLIES
1313 WALPOLE ROAD
STRAWBERRY HILL, PA 00000
www.Gothicglass.com 000.111.2222 (phone)
000.111.2222 (fax)

September 15, 2002

Ms. Carla Montoya
Valley Craft Stores
153 Hacienda Place
Houston, TX 00000

Dear Ms. Montoya:

We are pleased to inform you that your financial statement fully meets our standards of acceptability for a $10,000 line of credit, as you requested. The Luminous Lite stocked display case that you ordered pending the granting of credit has been shipped to you today by Leone Trucking. Your account has been billed for product cost and shipping charges of $2,726.32. An invoice is enclosed.

Gothic Glass now counts Valley Craft Stores among its valued customers. This means that you only need to pay 50 percent of your bill upon receipt of your merchandise, with the balance payable at our regular terms of 1.5 percent 10 days, net 45. A smooth relationship over the next twenty-four months will double your credit line at that time, should you so desire. As a Gothic Glass credit-line customer, you will receive advanced word of all sales and specials.

Thank you for your confidence in Gothic Glass. We pride ourselves on our quality products. Please feel free to call if you have any questions or check our online catalog at www.Gothicglass.com.

Sincerely,

Walt Hozak,
Credit Manager

Enclosures
invoice #334A-2
catalogue
order forms

Credit Inquiry Letter (form letter)

A company may use a form letter in response to an application for credit. It politely acknowledges the receipt of the order that accompanies the request, describes credit terms, and asks for a financial statement. This letter may be kept as a file in your word-processing software.

Purpose

1. To acknowledge the receipt of a customer's order and credit request

2. To request a financial statement

3. To establish a cordial relationship

Form

Introduction

- acknowledge receipt of order and credit request

- express pleasure at beginning a new business relationship

Body

- describe credit terms

- request financial statement

Conclusion

- encourage more business

FONTANA FURNITURE
533 VENTURA BOULEVARD
LOS ANGELES, CA 00000
Ph: 000.111.2222
Fax: 000.111.2222

_____
(date)

_____

_____

_____
(inside address)

Dear_____:

Our shipping department has passed to us the credit request that accompanies your purchase order number _____, dated _____, for _____. We are pleased to open your account and look forward to doing business with you.

Credit terms at Fontana Furniture are 10 percent on receipt of shipment, net 30 days. We are glad to open lines of credit with each customer whose financial statement passes our review. Would you please send or fax us your statement so that we can process it and proceed with your order?

Fontana Furniture appreciates your business, and please let us know how we can be of service to you.

Sincerely,

_____
Credit Office

Error Letter (mistake in billing)

This letter notifies a company that you have received a bill that contains an error. It should state the facts clearly and forthrightly and avoid reprimands. A photocopy of the erroneous bill may be included. This letter may be as short as two or three sentences.

Purpose

1. To inform the correspondent of an error in billing

2. To detail the error and note correction

Form

Introduction

▩ identify the bill

Body

▩ note the nature of the error

Conclusion

▩ stipulate the sum actually owed

▩ request a corrected invoice

THE RED WOK
133 Canal Street, New York, NY 00000
000.111.2222

7 February, 2002

Pieter Vanderhoven
Consolidated Restaurant Supply
115 East Fourteenth Street
New York, NY 00000

Dear Mr. Vanderhoven:

We have just received a Consolidated bill (No.677-211), dated 30 January 2002, in the amount of $123.50, for fifty place settings of Deluxe Baroque Flatware.

We believe this bill is in error. Please consult our purchase order number 342-C. We requested and were shipped the Standard model, which lists for $93.50 in your catalogue, page 52.

The flatware we have received is entirely satisfactory. We will submit payment upon receipt of a corrected invoice.

Sincerely,

Ting Ho, Manager

encl

Error Letter (mistake in payment)

This letter notifies a customer that a mistake has been made in paying a bill. It should be tactful and courteous without admonishing the customer. The letter should describe the error and the means of correction and assure the reader of your company's goodwill.

Purpose

1. To note an error in payment

2. To request a correction of the problem

Form

Introduction

▦ acknowledge the effort to pay

Body

▦ specify nature of error

▦ suggest means to rectify mistake

Conclusion

▦ assure reader of ongoing business relationship

ARIZONA FINANCIAL SERVICES

23 Federal Highway, Flagstaff AZ 00000
www.AFS.com
000.111.2222 (phone)
000.111.2222 (fax)

April 23, 2002

Boulevard Management
3373 Pico Boulevard
Los Angeles, CA 00000

ATTENTION: Linda Gomez

Madam:

We are grateful for your prompt payment by check of our invoice #44522 in the amount of $11,750.00 for 100 shares of Promex Communication common stock.

We regret that a missing endorsement signature has caused our bank to refuse payment on your draft. Would you please either endorse the enclosed check or send us a new draft and return it to us by express mail?

We trust that this matter can be corrected promptly, and we look forward to future transactions.

Sincerely,

Anthony Valente

Accountant Representative

hb

encl

Fundraising Letter

A nonprofit organization employs a fundraising letter to solicit money from potential donors. A fundraising letter should be honest and direct in expressing its request. It should be well reasoned, documenting the need to be filled, but it should also appeal to the reader's emotions.

Purpose

1. To inform the reader of a need

2. To motivate the reader to donate money

Introduction

▪ acknowledge the reader as a concerned person

▪ introduce the charitable cause

Body

▪ build a case for the cause with details and examples

▪ engage the reader's emotion

Conclusion

▪ thank reader for interest

▪ make request for funds

Nathan Foundation
121 Marcella Road
Denville, NJ 00000
000.000.0000

January 12, 2002

Dear Friend,

An education is the passport to success. For twenty-five years, the Nathan Foundation has dedicated itself to ensuring that students who fall below the poverty line will have the same opportunity for higher education as other Americans. The Nathan Foundation is launching a challenge that will match, dollar for dollar, donations made by July 1, 2002.

As the cost of a college education soars, many able students find themselves unable to realize their potential. Tuition has risen higher than the rate of inflation, and a four-year undergraduate education at many colleges now costs more than $100,000! The Nathan Foundation has provided scholarship assistance to deserving inner-city children to achieve their dreams. Nearly 400 students have been assisted, and our record speaks for itself. Among these students are lawyers, physicians, teachers, and entrepreneurs who are all productive citizens. Consider Dr. Tanya Jones, a former high-school drop out, who turned her life around as a Nathan Foundation Scholar. She now serves as associate professor of radiology at Upstate Medical School. Or Luis Lopes, raised by a single mother in public housing. He graduated *summa cum laude* from Ivy University and is now attending Gloria University Law School. There are more students in need like Tanya and Luis. Won't you open the doors of education to them?

The Nathan Foundation would like to help even more students who have overcome environments that marked them for failure and have achieved outstanding success. They need your help. Please fill out the enclosed pledge card and donate as generously as you can. Remember, your gift will be doubled if made before July 1!

Yours truly,

Vic Collabelli
Director

Inquiry Letter (solicited)

A solicited letter of inquiry is written in response to either a personal request or a public advertisement. You may have received the inquiry through a phone call, a newspaper advertisement, or perhaps an invitation to bid or submit a proposal. The letter should recall to the reader the specific details of the solicitation and state the reasons why you are making an inquiry.

Purpose

1. To acquire information

2. To respond to the reader's request

Form

Introduction

▪ recall the nature and date of the solicitation

Body

▪ describe specific situation or grounds of inquiry

▪ specify data needed

Conclusion

▪ state interest in further transactions

▪ express thanks for invitation to respond

FRANCONA ART /21 Indian Blvd./Lewisburg, PA 00000
www.Franconart.com/000.111.2222

27 May 2002

Mr. Frank Petraka
Executive Director
The Bloch Foundation
122 Valley Drive
Sunbury, PA 00000

Dear Mr. Petraka:

I received your letter dated 23 May requesting local artists to submit proposals for artwork in The Bloch Foundation headquarters currently under
construction in Sunbury.

Francona Art represents twelve regional artists. We have exclusive rights
to show and sell their works. We would be glad to meet with representatives
of

The Bloch Foundation to show you the range and depth of these artists. Their
styles range from abstract to representational and they work in a variety
of media. Our Web site, www.Franconart.com, contains a portfolio of graphic
works for your review.

Please call our office directly at 000.1111, extension 222, or fax your reply to 000.1111.

Sincerely,

Bruno Francona

ac
encl

Inquiry Letter (solicited, follow up)

This letter is written as a reminder if your first letter of solicitation has not been answered. It seeks to obtain a response where the original letter failed. It should be cordial and specific, trying to gain the reader's cooperation.

Purpose

1. To elicit an answer from an unresponsive correspondent

2. To show that the writer is still interested

Form

Introduction

■ review the situation

Body

■ suggest possible reasons for the absence of response

■ supply more relevant data

■ express hope that the response will be forthcoming

Conclusion

■ emphasize mutual benefit

■ express appreciation for reader's attention

FRANCONA ART /21 Indian Blvd./Lewisburg, PA 00000
www.Franconart.com/000.111.2222

9 June 2002

Mr. Frank Petraka
Executive Director
The Bloch Foundation
122 Valley Drive
Sunbury, PA 00000

Dear Mr. Petraka:

We wrote you two weeks ago in answer to your inquiry of 23 May soliciting artwork for your new headquarters building in Sunbury. Francona Art would be very interested in working with you.

We realize that your inquiry requested proposals directly from individual artists. Francona Art has exclusive rights to represent over a dozen local artists, and we cannot in fairness give favor to any one. We would be only too glad to have you visit our gallery or Web site, www.Franconart.com. If you prefer, we could send you transparencies of our artists' works. At that point we would be glad to facilitate any arrangement between you and the artist.

We do hope to hear from you soon. We know that The Bloch Foundation has contributed generously to artistic and educational institutions in the Buffalo Valley. By purchasing works from Francona Art, the Foundation will help support local artists and provide a showcase for them.

We thank you for your consideration and look forward to hearing from you.

Sincerely,

Bruno Francona

et

Inquiry Letter (unsolicited)

Businesses use a letter of inquiry to seek new customers, test the market, or obtain information. Frequently, a business sends an unsolicited letter of inquiry as a sales letters to potential customers.

Purpose

1. To obtain information on the price of goods or services

2. To start or continue a business relationship

Form

Introduction

▨ state reason for inquiry

Body

▨ explain why the reader has been selected as subject of inquiry

▨ describe in detail the information requested

Conclusion

▨ extend thanks for the assistance

CHEZ LILAH CHOCOLATS
213 FRENCH ROAD   SAN DIEGO, CA 00000
phone: (000) 111-2222 fax: (000) 111-2222
www.ChezLilah.com

December 27, 2002

Swanson Sweets
2912 Highway 70 East
Del Mar, CA 00000

Dear Sir or Madam:

Subject: Chocolate bars

Chez Lilah Chocolats is seeking retail outlets for its line of award-winning, artisan chocolate bars. For a limited time, we are offering independent merchants the opportunity to sell the finest chocolate bars available on the market.

As the premier chocolate maker in southern California, Chez Lilah uses only the highest-quality ingredients. We purchase the finest African and South American cacao beans. Our Le Plus Grand bittersweet bar consists of 85 percent cacao, and our Le Grand bar is 67 percent minimum. Compare the taste of our bars to the milk bars of our competitors, which contain no more than 33 percent cacao. We work only with natural ingredients, not the artificial powders, emulsifiers, and flavors found even in high-priced products. Chez Lilah Chocolat bars are priced to sell about 10 percent below most major brands so that independent retail stores can compete with discount and catalogue merchants. We can also package the chocolate with your logo and brand name, if you so desire.

Please contact our office, and we will arrange for our sales representative to call on you. She will be glad to explain our terms, discount, and sales policies.

Sincerely,

Lilah LaDouce

President

LL/ss
Encl: Catalogue

Inquiry Letter (negative answer)

If the answer to an inquiry is "no", the letter of denial should still maintain a positive tone that shows sensitivity to the reader.

Purpose

1. To inform the reader that his or her request is denied

2. To encourage the reader's goodwill

3. To suggest means to correct the situation

Form

Introduction

■ establish rapport with reader

Body

■ cite relevant information

■ inform the reader politely that the answer is "no"

Conclusion

■ try to suggest further possibilities

■ give support to the reader

MANUEL ALTERNATORS
311 Johnson Avenue
Davis, CA 00000
Ph: 000-111-2222
Fax: 000-111-2222

October 16, 2002

Ms. Linda Calabria
34 Stackhouse Drive
Wallace, NC 00000

Dear Ms. Calabria:

I thank you for your phone call of October 14, and especially for informing us of potential wiring problems with the Model X alternator. Our production staff is now reinspecting all units, and we are reviewing our assembly procedures.

As you know, the alternator comes with a 90-day warranty for parts only. Montross stands fully behind our product, but we cannot honor obligations beyond these limits and still offer our unit at a competitive price. Therefore, I regret that we cannot reimburse you for labor costs as you have requested.

The Model X is an extremely dependable unit, and I am sure that it will offer you many years of reliable use. Please call me if you have any further questions about your alternator.

Cordially,

Adam Morrison
Customer Relations

Inquiry Letter (positive answer)

Inquiries concern a wide variety of requests for information, products, or services. If the answer to an inquiry is "yes," then maintain a positive and encouraging tone.

Purpose

1. To inform the reader of a positive answer to a request

2. To explain reasons for the decision

Form

Introduction

▨ make a favorable response

Body

▨ explain relevant facts

▨ cite reasons for choice

▨ encourage more communication or business

Conclusion

▨ express goodwill

▨ offer further assistance

MANAGEMENT INSTITUTE OF AMERICA
233 Hidden Valley Road, Athens, GA 00000
000.111.2222 phone WWW.MIA.COM 000.111.2222 fax

March 12, 2002

Mr. Jawad Scott
May & Felton
22 McCants Street
Jacksonville, FL 00000

Dear Mr. Scott:

We are pleased to inform that you have been accepted into MIA's 2002 Executive Seminar. As you know, MIA is able to accommodate only a small number of the many applicants who apply for this annual program. Your application was an especially strong one, and we are pleased to have you with us. The seminar will be held on June 5, at the Riverside Resort Hotel in Athens.

The 2002 Executive Seminar promises to be an outstanding program. The Saturday morning session will focus on "climbing the corporate ladder" and will feature several well-known motivational speakers. The keynote address at the luncheon will be delivered by Dr. Frank Percovich, the distinguished economist from the Free Enterprise Foundation. The afternoon program will feature a career-development panel titled Tools of Trade, followed by small group workshops. We will wrap up the seminar with a cocktail party and banquet.

We thank you again for your interest in the Executive Seminar. Your place will be guaranteed upon receipt of the $750 registration fee, which includes food, lodging, and airport transportation. We would appreciate your completing the enclosed forms. If you have any questions, please call me at 1.800.111.2222. Look forward to seeing you June 5!

Sincerely,

June Chung
Administrative Director

Enclosures

Introduction Letter

A letter of introduction attests to the financial integrity and good character of the person who bears it. While it may be hand-delivered by the person described in the letter, a letter of introduction faxed or mailed allows the reader to make arrangements prior to the person's arrival.

Purpose

1. To establish the personal, corporate, or financial integrity of the person described in the letter

2. To arrange the meeting of potential associates

3. To establish that the meeting will benefit all parties

Form

Introduction

■ present the person to the correspondent

■ describe relationship to the writer

Body

■ detail the person's qualifications

■ state reasons to meet the person

Conclusion

■ assert the personal or financial integrity of the person

FIRST NATIONAL BANK OF COLUMBUS
123 MAIN STREET
COLUMBUS, GEORGIA 00000
000-111-2222

6 October, 2002

Mr. Robert Hernandez, Vice President
Southeastern Bancorp
500 Bank Plaza
Atlanta, Georgia 00000

Dear Mr. Hernandez:

I write to introduce you to William Lakes, President of Star Electronics and a member of our Board of Directors since 1983.

Mr. Lakes and his firm have maintained an excellent credit rating with First National for 24 years. He will be in Atlanta on November 4 to attend the Consumer Electronics Convention. If he has need of banking services during his stay, the First National Bank of Columbus requests that every courtesy be extended to him. We vouch for his good character and financial integrity.

Please call me personally if you have any further questions or need to have his credit verified.

Sincerely,

First National Bank of Columbus

Ella M. Snipes
President

ES/kt

Invitation Letter (formal)

This letter extends an invitation on behalf of a person or a firm. It should be graceful, polite, and specific. The reader should be told why he or she has been invited, as well as where and when the event will be held. This letter may be as short as three sentences.

Purposes

1. To extend an invitation

2. To encourage the reader to accept

Form

Introduction

■ state time and place of the event

■ invite the person or a representative of the firm

Body

■ explain why the invitation has been extended

Conclusion

■ express hope for a positive answer

ELSID Truck Sales
36 Germantown Avenue
Charleston, South Carolina 00000
(000) 111-2222

February 3, 2002

Mr. Joe Brown Sr., Vice President
Regal Motor Freight
101 Fall Drive
Columbia, South Carolina 00000

Dear Mr. Brown:

ELSID Truck Sales invites you to an exclusive showing of the new Davis Electric Delivery Van. The presentation will take place at a luncheon at The Towers, 2107 Vista Parkway, Charleston, at 12:00 on February 21. We hope that you will be able to attend.

ELSID Truck Sales is the sole regional sales agent for the Davis line. As you well know, recent technological advances have made electrically powered vehicles increasingly attractive to commercial users. The Davis offers reliability with superb economy, and it exceeds all state and federal environmental standards.

We are certain the Davis delivery van can improve your service and your profits. We look forward to seeing you. Just call our office at 000-0000 and we will be glad to secure a place for you.

Sincerely,

ELSID Transportation Services

Julian Gorden, Sales Manager

Invitation Letter (informal)

An informal invitation is courteous and gracious, but brief. The letter should describe the occasion and express the host's wish to have the reader attend. The tone will be friendlier and more personal than that of a formal invitation.

Purpose

1. To invite the correspondent to an event

2. To motivate the person to attend

Form

Introduction

■ state where and when the event is to occur

■ extend the invitation

Body

■ describe the reason for the invitation

Closing

■ express the hope that the person will attend

```
ELSID Truck Sales
36 Germantown Avenue
Charleston, South Carolina   00000
(000) 111-2222
```

February 3, 2002

Mr. Joe Brown, Vice President
Regal Motor Freight
101 Fall Drive
Columbia, South Carolina 00000

Dear Joe,

We're giving a luncheon at The Towers at 12:00 on March 21 to introduce the Davis electric delivery van. We hope you'll be able to come.

As I mentioned to you at last week's Chamber of Commerce meeting, we have secured the regional franchise for the Davis line. I think you'll agree that the Davis represents a technological breakthrough, and I think you'll find it most interesting.

Best,

Julian Gorden

Invitation Letter (accepting)

A letter of acceptance should be short and gracious. It expresses interest in the event and gratitude for the invitation. A one- or two-sentence note may be sufficient.

Purpose

1. To accept an invitation

2. To show appreciation

Form

Introduction

▓ state that you accept

Body

▓ express interest

▓ repeat time and place

Conclusion

▓ thank reader for thoughtfulness

REGAL MOTOR FREIGHT
101 FALL DRIVE
COLUMBIA, SC 00000

February 7, 2002

Mr. Julian Gorden
Sales Agent
ELSID Truck Sales
36 Germantown Avenue
Charleston, South Carolina 00000

Dear Mr. Gorden:

I've examined your sales literature and appreciate your invitation to take a closer look at the Davis truck line. Our firm is very interested in electric delivery vans, and I would like to see what you have to offer.

Thanks for the invitation, and I look forward to meeting you at The Towers on 21 February.

Sincerely,

Joe Brown, Sr.
Vice President

www.RMF.com   000.111.2222 (phone)   000.111.2222 (fax)

Invitation (declined)

This letter expresses the writer's regrets over an inability to accept an invitation. It should be succinct but polite. The writer may wish to offer an explanation. A few sentences should be adequate.

Purpose

1. To decline an invitation

2. To convey regret

Form

Introduction

■ acknowledge the invitation

Body

■ comment on value of the invitation

■ explain why it must be declined

■ state regret

Conclusion

■ express thanks for invitation

■ extend wishes for a successful event

REGAL MOTOR FREIGHT
101 FALL DRIVE
COLUMBIA, SC 00000

February 7, 2002

Mr. Julian Gorden
Sales Agent
ELSID Truck Sales
36 Germantown Avenue
Charleston, South Carolina 00000

Dear Julian:

I appreciate your sending me the literature on your electric delivery vans and inviting me to the presentation at The Towers on February 21. However, our firm does long-distance shipping exclusively, and we need trucks with capabilities well beyond the limited mileage range of electric delivery vans.

If we do decide to offer local delivery service, we will be sure to contact you. We wish you good luck with the Davis line and thank you for thinking of us.

Sincerely,

Joe Brown, Sr.
Vice President

sdg

www.RMF.com   000.111.2222 (phone)   000.111.2222 (fax)

Motivational Letter

A letter of motivation encourages employees to increase their productivity.

Purpose

1. To praise an outstanding employee and encourage further excellence

2. To inspire an employee who is not performing up to standards

Form

Introduction

■ establish a positive tone

■ find something to praise

Body

■ show appreciation of accomplishments

■ note obstacles overcome

■ suggest means to improve

Conclusion

■ urge continued good work and effort

Piedmont Life and Casualty
701 Latta Road
Gretna, VA 00000
Phone: 000 111-2222   www.piedmont.net
Fax: 000 111-2222

August 19, 2002

Karl Eckerman
211 Athens Street
Danville, VA 00000

Dear Karl:

This month marks the completion of your first year as our sales agent in Danville. We appreciate the long hours and hard work that you have dedicated to building a customer base there. You have an exemplary record, and the firm appreciates your efforts.

With the economic downturn of the past few months the entire insurance industry has been hurt. We hope that you will not feel discouraged if your first-year results did not meet your expectations. We feel assured that your efforts are building a foundation for future sales, and your commissions will climb accordingly. Business forecasts are sounding more optimistic, and we look forward to improved sales figures as the economy improves. The Southeast remains one of the fastest growing regions of the country.

Please know that Piedmont Life and Casualty appreciates how well you are representing us. We value you as an employee and look forward to productive years ahead. Let us know if we can help you in any way.

Yours truly,

Jack McCloskey
Regional Sales Manager

Order Letter

An order letter requests goods or services. "Please send" is the standard opening. Companies routinely use standard forms in place of letters, and the order may be sent by fax. Increasingly, orders may be placed by e-mail through a Web site.

Purpose

1. To place a written order for goods or services

2. To confirm in writing an order made by person or by telephone

Form

Introduction

■ state directly and in detail the goods or services requested

Body

■ indicate relevant data as to quantity, size, color, or style

■ cite identifying information such as serial number, catalogue page, or advertised source

■ indicate unit price, subtotal cost, and total sum and method of payment

■ include shipping information

Conclusion

■ briefly thank the person or department for attentive service

GRECO HARDWARE 2113 Atlantic Avenue Brooklyn NY 00000
Web site: grecohardware.com
Phone: 000.111.2222
Fax: 000.111.2222

June 6, 2002

Catalogue Sales Department
Crown Supply
889 Hillary Parkway
Thomasville, NC 0000

Dear Sir or Madam:

Please sent the following items listed in your Specialty Items Supplement, page 14, of your 2002 catalogue:

1 box (50 count)	TB1199 1" stainless steel cotter pins	@$5.75	$5.75
2 boxes (25 count)	TB1207 2" stainless steel cotter pins	@ 4.75	9.50
			$14.75

Please bill our account Number GH7771. Ship priority mail.

Thank you for your prompt service.

Sincerely,

Jose Pepe

Order Letter (follow up)

If an order is not received or satisfactorily filled, then a follow-up letter may be sent. The letter should refer by date and invoice number to the original order, describing the goods in detail. Specify what remedial action should be taken.

Purpose

1. To remind a supplier of an order

2. To motivate the supplier to fill the order or offer a satisfactory explanation

Form

Introduction

■ review history of the order

Body

■ request the filling of the order

■ explain reasons for urgency

Conclusion

■ request refund or adjustment if order cannot be filled

■ express confidence in supplier's good intentions

SENECA UNIVERSITY STUDENT STORES
BOX 112
SENECA, NY 00000
www.senecau.edu
000.111.2222

7 August 2002

Pathway Industries
333 Keever Drive
St. Louis, MO 00000

Dear Sir or Madam:

Subject: Invoice no. 10566-NC

On 25 May 2002, Student Stores order 1,000 ballpoint pens with the Seneca University logo imprinted. The order included our check for $249.50 for cost and shipping. We were promised delivery within 60 days.

We have not yet received shipment of the pens. We need them urgently to augment a public-relations campaign for the University's football team. If shipment cannot be arranged immediately, please inform us of the problem and the possible shipping date.

If the order cannot be filled, then please refund our payment. We appreciate your prompt attention

Sincerely,

Toni Walker
Manager

ds

Order Letter (filled and shipped, form letter)

This form letter confirms the receipt of an order and informs the customer of shipping arrangements. This letter may consist of a preprinted form that may be kept on file in your computer. This form may be sent by fax or by e-mail.

Purpose

1. To acknowledge receipt of an order

2. To note shipment of goods

Form

Introduction

▪ state customer's invoice number, order date, description of goods

Body

▪ state date shipped

Conclusion

▪ express goodwill to customer

BOULDER CAMPING SUPPLIES
112 Rocky Road
Glenwood Springs, CO 00000
000 111-2222 (phone)   000 111-22222 (fax)   www.bouldercamp.net

_____
(date)

_____
_____
_____
(inside address)

Dear _____:

Your order number _____, dated_____, for
_____ _____, was received by
us on _____.

Your merchandise was shipped on _____.

We appreciate your business. Please let us know if the merchandise does not
meet your satisfaction.

Sincerely,

_____
Shipping agent

Order Letter (out of stock, form letter)

This form letter is sent to customers when your firm is unable to fill an order because the item is out of stock. It should seek to maintain the customer's business and goodwill. This letter, too, may consist of a preprinted form and may be faxed or e-mailed to the customer.

Purpose

1. To inform a customer that the order cannot be filled immediately

2. To motivate the customer to wait

Form

Introduction

■ acknowledge receipt of the order

Body

■ explain that goods are unavailable

■ state date of anticipated shipment

Conclusion

■ express regret at inconvenience

■ encourage continued business

THE YARN BROKERS
65 Attermeier Drive
Milwaukee, WI 00000
000.111.2222

_____
(date)

_____

_____

_____
(inside address)

Dear _____:

We received your order number _____for
_____ _____ on
_____.

We regret that this order cannot be filled immediately, as we are tempo-
rarily out of stock. We anticipate shipping the merchandise to you by
_____.

We regret any inconvenience this delay may have caused. We appreciate your
business and look forward to serving you in the future.

Sincerely,

_____
Shipping

Political Action Letter

A letter is frequently sent to government officials to support or oppose legislation or actions that affect a business directly or the business climate generally. The letter should be specific and build a strong factual case. Do not threaten, but you may remind the official of the consequences of his or her position. A courteous tone is most effective.

Purpose

1. To support or oppose a specific policy or legislation

2. To convince the official to act in your behalf

3. To request assistance on a particular problem

Form

Introduction

▓ cite the specific law or action

▓ state support or opposition

Body

▓ explain reasons for your stand

▓ cite facts and figures

▓ point to popular support for your position

Conclusion

▓ remind official of the consequences of his or her position

▓ thank official for considering your opinion

▓ ask for a response

RHODES TRAVEL SOUTH SQUARE MALL SANDUSKY OH 00000
E-mail: rhodes@net.comPhone: 000-111-2222   Fax: 000-111-2222

2 March 2002

The Honorable Powell Ketchum
2345 Longworth HOB
Washington, DC 00000

Sir:

As president of Rhodes Travel, I urge you to oppose HR 3567 now being considered by the Ways and Means Committee. I believe the proposed excise tax on international airline tickets will seriously harm an already threatened industry.

Passenger loads have dropped almost 30 percent in the past twelve months, and a generally depressed economy has reduced international travel. Near-empty planes are commonplace. A surtax now will only discourage travel. The airline industry has been troubled by increasing labor and fuel costs. Since deregulation, competition has lowered profit margins. The big three carriers reported record losses totaling $3.5 billion for the 2001 fiscal year. We need to create incentives for people to travel, not burden them with more penalties. HR 3567 is opposed not only by the travel industry and its professional associations, but also by labor and aircraft manufacturers.

The travel industry is a major employer that contributes billions in taxes and generates millions of jobs. We hope that the government would support us rather than add to our problems.

It is in the best interest of the country for HR 3567 to be shelved. I look forward to hearing your position on this issue.

Sincerely,

Gus Mamoulian
President

Recommendation Letter

A letter of recommendation offers an evaluation of an employee or colleague who is applying for another position. Your evaluation may determine whether the person is hired or not, so measure your words carefully. A person may be highly recommended, recommended, or recommended with qualifications. This letter may be written generally to be kept on file or written specifically for a particular position.

Purpose

1. To provide personal and professional background on an employee or colleague

2. To evaluate the candidate's qualifications for another job

Form

Introduction

- state the applicant's name and position applied for

- indicate briefly your recommendation

Body

- explain your relationship to the candidate

- define the applicant's strengths and weaknesses

- describe the person's abilities and accomplishments

- indicate the candidate's potential for growth

Conclusion

- summarize your evaluation

- urge reader to give applicant serious consideration

- offer to be available for further comment

PARKER INSURANCE AGENCY
112 Kupfer Boulevard
Brenda, OR 00000
000.111.2222

July 23, 2002

Mr. Hatem Mansoor
Personnel Department
Ginsburg Department Stores
313 Cameron Avenue
Eugene, OR 00000

Dear Mr. Mansoor:

I am happy to recommend Wilsonia Peebles, who has applied for a sales position with Ginsburg Department Stores.

Ms. Peebles has worked under my supervision for three years as a receptionist and account secretary with our agency. She has maintained our files, handled billings, and kept records for several hundred accounts. I have always found her to be efficient, accurate, and honest.

Although she has not had experience with retail sales in our firm, we have found her to be pleasant and helpful when working with our customers. She has shown herself to be a quick learner who works well independently.

I will be sorry to lose Ms. Peebles, but I understand her desire to find a position closer to her home that can offer her more flexible hours. I think that you would be quite fortunate to have her on your staff, and I heartily recommend her.

Sincerely,

Linda Stuart
Office Manager

pc

Refund Letter

A refund letter informs correspondents that you are crediting them for an over-payment for goods or services. Emphasize your company's reliability and promptness in correcting the problem. A corrected invoice may be included.

Purpose

1. To inform the customer of an error and state how refund will be made

2. To retain the customer's confidence

Form

Introduction

▪ indicate amount of refund or correct cost

Body

▪ offer apology for any inconvenience

▪ indicate how the reimbursement is being paid or credited

Conclusion

▪ express appreciation for the customer's business

▪ offer to answer any questions

ENGLISH STATIONERS
5 Abbey Road
Dylan, OR 00000
000.111.2222   **www.englishst.net**

7 February 2002

Mr. Shane Joyce
Michael Novelty Company
113 Wilmington Way
Lumberton, NC 00000

Dear Mr. Joyce:

Subject: Purchase Order 533-A

An audit of your account confirms that the correct cost of the business forms that you ordered on January 5, 2002, is $70.80.

Thank you for calling this matter to our attention. We apologize for any inconvenience this error has caused you. Your account has been amended to show a credit of $8.80, as requested in your letter of February 2.

A corrected invoice for $70.80 accompanies this letter. We value your business and look forward to serving you in the future. Please call me if you have any questions.

Sincerely,

Thelma Arthur
Billing Department

unc

encl.

Request Letter

A letter of request asks for information about products or services.

Purpose

1. To obtain information

2. To motivate reader to respond quickly and efficiently

Form

Introduction

▓ make request for specific information

Body

▓ state your requirements as to rates, dates, or other needs

Conclusion

▓ express appreciation for rapid reply

▓ suggest possible benefits to the reader

WOLVERINE FINANCIAL SERVICES 311 Bank Street   Detroit, MI 00000

May 27, 2002

Laurel Hill Conference Center
36 Winding Hill Road
Laurel Hill, MI 00000

Dear Sir or Madam:

Could you please send us literature on the Laurel Hill Conference Center?
We would appreciate any material that illustrates the Center's facilities
and its setting. Please also include a rate schedule.

We are in the preliminary stages of selecting a site for our annual staff
retreat that will be held on a Saturday in September, 2003. We will need
facilities that can accommodate 60 people for the one-day meeting. We will
require at least three seminar rooms as well as catering facilities.

We hope to make a final selection of the site by July 1, so we appreciate your
prompt reply. I will be glad to meet with your sales agent after reviewing
your literature.

Sincerely,

Robert Sekora
Vice President

PN

ph: 000.111.2222 – fax: 000.111.2222 – www.wolverine.org

Reservation Letter

This letter makes or confirms a reservation for travel, facilities, or accommodations. It may be sent by fax or by e-mail.

Purpose

1. To secure or confirm reservations

2. To affirm length of stay

3. To request special arrangements

Form

Introduction

■ state number in party and name on reservation

■ specify type of accommodations

■ specify length of stay

Body

■ state arrival and departure times and dates

■ explain special needs

Conclusion

■ indicate amount and method of payment

■ request written confirmation

THE JACKSON CLINIC
511 LAKE LENORE ROAD
JACKSON, MS 00000
000.111.2222

March 19, 2002

Gateway Hotel
83 Palisades Avenue
San Diego, CA 00000

Dear Sir or Madam:

Please reserve a room for April 15 and 16 for Dr. Percy Walker who will be attending the Society of Family Practitioners Convention.

Dr. Walker will arrive after 1:00 PM on Friday, April 15, and will be checking out after the final session on Sunday, April 17. Dr. Walker would prefer a non-smoking room with a king-size bed.

We understand the convention rate is $129. Full payment will be made with our corporate Bankfast credit card #000 111 222 333, expiration 05/04. Please send us confirmation at your earliest convenience.

Sincerely,

Jenna Leid
Office Manager

Resignation Letter

A letter of resignation should be firm and businesslike, whatever the reason for leaving. State your determination to leave and briefly outline reasons. Acknowledge those who were helpful to you and express appreciation for the job. The reader may be called to recommend you when you apply for a new position.

Purpose

1. To announce your intention to resign

2. To explain reasons for quitting

Form

Introduction

▪ declare that you are leaving

▪ state effective date

Body

▪ briefly explain reasons for quitting

▪ thank employer for cooperation

Conclusion

▪ express best wishes for future success

17-A Broadway Apartments

Durham, NH 00000

September 12, 2002

Mr. Harold LeBow
Smith & Guthridge
32 Ram Plaza
Greenville, NH 00000

Dear Mr. LeBow:

I wish to inform you that I will resign my position as sales agent on January 1.

Having worked with Smith & Guthridge for four years, I have enjoyed my association with you and the staff. I have decided, however, to return to Boston to join the family business.

Working at Smith & Guthridge has been an important learning experience for me. I hope that I have contributed to the firm's success, and I wish you continued good fortune in the future.

Sincerely,

Irene McLeod

Sales Letter

Business correspondence tends to follow fairly standard forms, but sales letters have no rules except to succeed in winning sales of goods or services. The two sample sales letters that follow represent two basic types: the dramatic or "hard-sell" letter and the more restrained "soft-sell" letter. All good sales letters establish a friendly, conversational tone. They appeal to the emotions, but they also use testimonials, expert opinion, and independent test results to appeal to the reader's logic. Good sales letters anticipate objections and lead the reader through the sales presentation with rhetorical questions. The hard-sell letter differs from the soft-sell letter by tending toward emotional appeal and by exploiting graphics, typefaces, and punctuation to emphasize the sales pitch. Word-processing systems allow individual addressing of mass mailings of sales letters.

Purpose

1. To build direct sales business

2. To locate leads or encourage inquiries

3. To announce a new product and create a market

4. To secure new dealers or invigorate existing ones

Form

Introduction

■ capture reader's attention with a question, quotation, or dramatic statement

Body

■ create a desire for the product or service

■ convince the reader of its value

Conclusion

■ encourage action for the sale

■ make it convenient for the reader to buy or inquire further

**SAFECO SECURITY SYSTEMS 11 Elm Road Peoria, IL 00000
000 111-2222 / www.safeco.net**

Do you feel comfortable, Mr. Savio, reading about **house burglaries** day after day in our local newspapers. Are you aware that criminals have **stolen an estimated $3,000,000** from homes in the Peoria area alone in the past 12 months!

Do you feel **secure** in your own home? Is your house **protected** from the professional criminal?   FBI statistics indicate that across the country one **breaking-and-entering** crime is reported, on the average, every 15 minutes, day and night.

Would a burglar find your house an inviting target? If you were a burglar, would you break into a home knowing that it is hot wired to the police? Or would you look elsewhere?

I think that you'll agree that knowing how to make your house more **secure** is the best **protection** that you can give to your family and possessions.

We at **SAFECO SECURITY SYSTEMS** would like to have one of our **Home Security Agents** speak to you about how to make your home **safe** from even the most experienced burglar. The Agent will be glad to give your home a free security inspection and leave with you, at no obligation, our **home security** booklet, *Who Says Your House is Safe?*

You'll learn

• what a master burglar looks for when he "cases a joint"
• how he determines the best time to break in
• how he finds your hiding places for cash, jewelry, and valuables
• HOW HE EVADES THOSE ALARM SYSTEMS YOU CAN BUY AT YOUR LOCAL DISCOUNT STORE

SAFECO SECURITY SYSTEMS are the finest, most technologically advanced units on the market. Our systems have been endorsed by the National Association of Security Officers and the Consumer Safety Society. They meet or exceed all industry standards. For the past 23 years, **SAFECO SECURITY SYSTEMS** have been **protecting** banks, factories, and retail stores across the Midwest.

SAFECO SECURITY SYSTEMS for the past three years has been making its **protective** devices available to you, the homeowner. We have already **protected** over 12,000 homes in the tristate area. Your **SAFECO SECURITY SYSTEM** will be custom installed and periodically serviced for your full protection.

Now, thanks to breakthroughs in microelectronics, we can offer you a **SAFECO SECURITY SYSTEM** at rates far lower than you would expect to pay for **complete protection for your home.**

Can you, Mr. Savio, put a price on **peace of mind**?

Mail the enclosed card today. You'll get a free valuable booklet, *Who Says Your House is Safe?* And a **free security inspection** of your home. All you have to do is check **YES** on the enclosed card. Or telephone us at 000-1111.

Chris Mills

President, **Safeco Security Systems**

P. S. For the first 100 customers who call, **Safeco Security Systems** will offer a 10 percent discount.

SAFECO SECURITY SYSTEMS 11 Elm Road Peoria, IL 00000
000 111-2222 / www.safeco.net

December 27, 2002

Mr. Frank Savio
101 McRider Avenue
Peoria, IL 00000

Dear Mr. Savio:

We at Safeco Security Systems want to acquaint you with a new product that
we are offering to help you make your home more secure. For the past 23
years, Safeco has been the leading commercial installer of security alarm
systems. We are now offering that same protection to homeowners in the
tristate area.

You are no doubt well aware of the dramatic rise in house burglaries. The
cost in the last 12 months in the Peoria area alone is estimated at $3,000,000.
According to FBI statistics, a breaking and entering is reported every 15
minutes, day and night, nationwide.

A Safeco Security System can be custom installed in your home at a price far
below what you would expect to pay. Recent technological advances in microelectronics have made these units even more affordable. They come with
an electronic alarm that will send a signal directly to your local police
department or security patrol. In the past three years alone, Safeco Security Systems has installed these home-protection devices in more than 12,000
homes.

Safeco units comply with all state and federal regulations and meet or exceed all industry standards. Our systems have been endorsed by the National
Association of Security Officers and the Consumer Safety Society.

Safeco Security Systems would be happy to have one of our Home Security
Agents speak to you at no obligation. The Agent will be glad to give you a
free home security inspection and leave for you, as a gift, a guidebook on
protecting your house, *Home Safe Home*. Just check "yes" on the enclosed
card or call our office at 000-1111 to arrange an appointment.

Sincerely,

Chris Mills
President

Season's Greetings

Season's greetings are sent to customers or associates to promote goodwill.
For Christmas especially, be as general as possible and sensitive to the religious
feelings of all your customers.

Purpose

1. To express holiday greetings

2. To thank customers for their loyalty

Form

Introduction

■ express holiday wishes

Body

■ thank reader for loyal patronage

Conclusion

■ extend personal greetings

OLYMPIA NATIONAL BANK
12 BRIDGE STREET OLYMPIC WA 00000
000.111.2222   www.olympia.net

December 15, 2002

Mrs. Virginia Nettles-King
23 Woodside Lane
Fords, WA 00000

Dear Mrs. Nettles-King,

We at Olympia National Bank want to express to you our best wishes at this
holiday season. We appreciate your patronage and look forward to serving
you in the future.

May the New Year bring you and your family health and happiness!

Yours truly,

Walter Petroski
President

Sympathy Letter

A letter of sympathy or condolence expresses close personal bonds. The salutation reflects the relationship between the writer and the customer or staff member being addressed. A letter of sympathy may be a one- or two-paragraph note. It can be handwritten if the recipient is a close friend.

Purpose

1. To express sympathy

2. To offer aid or assistance

Form

Introduction

■ acknowledge the loss

■ set a concerned tone

Body

■ offer support

Conclusion

■ express friendship

■ offer help

14 Saunders Road

Annapolis, MD 00000

October 30, 2002

Ms. Susan Barry

Chesapeake Investment Services

223 Kepley Road

Baltimore, MD 00000

Dear Susan,

I have just learned from Donna Haley that your mother recently passed away. I remember her as a very fine, warm person who always took an interest in the well being of others.

We at Jordan Lake Enterprises want you to know that we're thinking of you. If we can help you in any way, please call upon us. We'd also like to contribute to a charity of your choice in her memory. Let us know your preference.

Best wishes,

Jack Derrida

Transmittal Letter

A letter of transmittal introduces a report to readers outside of your company. Two or three sentences may be sufficient. A longer letter can offer a summary of the report, emphasizing its conclusions. Frequently, in-house reports will be accompanied by a memorandum of transmittal.

Purpose

1. To call attention to a formal report

2. To emphasize the findings of the report

3. To encourage reader's support and goodwill

Form

Introduction

- describe subject of report

- state reasons for its distribution

Body

- summarize the report or its most important finding

- state your opinion of the report's value

Conclusion

- thank correspondent for reading the report

- ask for a response in writing, by telephone, or in personal consultation

PARKLAND CONSULTANTS
88 FREDONIA ROAD
JONESBORO, TN 00000

September 9, 2002

Board of Commissioners
Franklin County
112 Main Street
Franklinton, TN 00000

Dear Commissioner:

We are pleased to submit to the Board of Commissioners the report on
Greenways in Franklin County.

Our planning staff, in consultation with the Citizens Advisory Board, has
studied the areas of concern requested by the Board in Resolution 3349,
passed January 12, 2002. We considered the site selection of a greenway in
terms of its environmental impact, recreational opportunities, alternative
transportation potential, and construction cost. We also studied state and
federal regulations on funding and handicapped access.

Our recommendation is that Franklin County build a greenway on the aban-
doned right of way of the Southeastern Railroad. We are confident that this
route will best protect the environment and serve the interests of the citizens of Franklin County. Please call us at Parkland Consultants if you have
any questions about any aspect of this study. We look forward to presenting
this report to the Board of Commissioners at its October 1 meeting.

Yours truly,

Frank Lineberger
President

Enclosure: Greenways in Franklin County
Copies: LaVon Williams William Rivers
Blanche DuBose   Janice Lopes
Theodore Capowski   Tommy Flaherty

Ph: (000) 111-2222 / Fax: (000) 111-2222 / www.parkland.net

Business Letter Checklist

❑ Letterhead or return address

❑ Dateline

❑ Confidential notation (optional)

❑ Mail notation (optional)

❑ Inside address

❑ Attention line (optional)

❑ Salutation

❑ Subject Line (optional)

❑ Introductory paragraph

❑ Body paragraph(s)

❑ Concluding paragraph

❑ Complimentary close

❑ Company name (optional)

❑ Signature

❑ Writer's name

❑ Title or position (optional)

❑ Identification initials (optional)

❑ Enclosure notation (optional)

❑ Carbon copy notation (optional)

❑ Postscript (optional)

❑ Mail notation (optional)

Chapter 2

Business Writing Style

In business writing, it is important to write clearly, avoiding jargon and wordiness. To achieve this, try to use fresh language without resorting to clichés. In addition, it is important to make your points in the fewest possible words.

Wordiness

Wordiness involves the use of dead words that do not contribute to the meaning of a sentence. Certain commonly used phrases are wordy and should be reduced or omitted. For example:

wordy: I need your help *in order to* solve the problem.

better: I need your help *to* solve the problem.

wordy: *Due to the fact* that the merchandise was damaged, we are withholding payment.

better: *Because* the merchandise was damaged, we are withholding payment.

wordy: *It is our opinion* that the policy should be changed.

better: *We feel* that the policy should be changed.

To follow is a list of wordy phrases with suggested corrections:

Wordy	Suggested Correction
at a later date	later
despite the fact that	although
due to the fact that	because
for the purpose of	for, to
in addition	also
in a number of cases	some
in order that	so
in order to	to
in reference to	about
in terms of	as for
in the amount of	for, of
in the event of	if
in the near future	soon
in this day and age	now, today
in view of	because, since
it is our opinion that	we feel
on the occasion of	when
prior to	before
subsequent to	after
without further delay	immediately
with reference to	about
with respect to	about
would you please be so kind as to	please

Redundancy

Redundancy is a form of wordiness. Redundant words repeat rather than develop the point. To describe something as brown in color is redundant since brown implies color. For example:

redundant: In *the year of 1994*, retail sales dropped sharply.
better: In *1994,* retail sales dropped sharply.

redundant: Suarez Mills is the *one and only* source of the fabric.
better: Suarez Mills is the *only* source of the fabric.

redundant: I enclose a check for *the amount of $378.25.*
better: I enclose a check for *$378.25.*

To follow are some redundant phrases with suggested improvements:

Redundant	Improved
agreeable and satisfactory	agreeable or satisfactory
and etc.	etc.
basic fundamentals	basics or fundamentals
completely perfect	perfect
consensus of opinion	consensus
each and every	each
first and foremost	first
follows after	follows
full and complete	full or complete
general consensus	consensus
hope and trust	hope or trust
if and when	if or when
in my personal opinion	in my opinion
insist and demand	insist or demand
meet together	meet
most unique	unique
one and only	only
prompt and speedy	prompt
repeats again	repeats
reverts back	reverts
right and proper	right or proper
sincere and earnest	sincere or earnest
thoughtful and considerate	thoughtful or considerate
true facts	facts
very unique	unique
willing and eager	willing or eager

Jargon

Jargon occurs when the writer uses excessively technical words, often very long ones, when simpler, shorter words would be more effective. Be wary of words that end in *-ize*, *-tion*, or *-ity*. Though writers of jargon try to demonstrate that they are authorities, they more often confuse the reader. For example:

jargon: An enhanced commitment to a public relations effort remains a viable option for the firm.
better: We may also wish to improve our public relations.

jargon: The implementation of cost-cutting strategies can impact budgetary deficits.
better: Cutting costs will reduce deficits.

Jargon can often be corrected by using more concrete words. To follow is a list of jargon:

acknowledge receipt of

answer affirmatively, negatively

expend maximum effort

feedback

impact a problem

implement a decision

input

interface

proactive

remunerate

Clichés

Clichés are expressions that have lost their meaning through overuse. Rather than request a 100-percent effort, ask for hard work. For example:

cliché: In today's market, we must *move forward or fall behind*.
better: In today's market, we must improve our efficiency.

cliché: The Prostar is *just what you're looking for*.
better: The Prostar will meet your word-processing needs.

Other clichés include:

allow me to	100-percent effort
along these lines	over the hill
do our utmost	pave the way
down, but not out	sell like hot cakes
facts of life	short and sweet
for your information	slow but sure
keep abreast	to be perfectly honest
last but not least	touch all bases
latest developments	vicious circle
meet the eye	work like a dog
nip in the bud	

Chapter 3

Numbers in Correspondence

Various style manuals offer different suggestions as to whether numbers should appear in a text as figures (*1, 2, 3, 4...*) or spelled out (*one, two, three, four...*). Check to see if your company has a policy, or you may follow these guidelines. The important point is to be consistent.

Spelled Out

1. Numbers under one hundred within the text:
   sixty-two people
   three times as large
   seven recommendations
   twenty-five numbers

2. Any number that begins a sentence:
   Nineteen ninety-eight was the company's best year.
   Two hundred forty workers were hired.

3. Centuries, round numbers, and indefinite expressions:
   hundreds of men
   a thousand reasons
   less than a million dollars
   the early seventies, but the 1970s
   the nineteenth century

4. Large numbers in very formal writing such as legal work:
   sixteen hundred and twenty
   exactly four thousand
   nineteen hundred and eighty-four

5. Fractions standing alone or followed by *of a* or *of an*:
   one-half inch
   three fourths of a pie
   one third of an acre

6. Ordinal numbers less than one hundred:
   twentieth century
   Fifth Fleet
   Eighty-second Congress
   Twelfth Avenue

Expressed in Figures

1. Numbers over one hundred within ordinary text:
   Enrollment reached 16,487
   952 ballots
   198 districts

2. All numbers in tables

3. Measurements of physical properties in scientific or technical writing, and any number used with a symbol or abbreviated unit of measurement:
   20/20 vision
   6 pounds
   $17 \frac{1}{2}''$
   43 mm
   13 lb. 2 oz.
   8:30 A.M.

4. Serial numbers, including numbers designating the pages and other parts of a book:
   Bulletin 756
   1900 Twenty-first Street
   pages 322-34
   diagram 4

5. Years:
   53 A.D.
   1965
   1255 B.C.E.
6. Fractions that would be awkward if spelled out:
   8 $\frac{1}{2}$-by-11-inch bond paper
7. Decimal fractions and percentages:
   10.5 percent return
   $83.95
   a grade point average of 3.42
8. All numbers referring to the same category in a single passage if the largest is over one hundred:
   Of the 137 delegates at the meeting, only 9 opposed the plan.

Large Numbers

Large numbers are usually expressed in figures; however, numbers from one million up that end in four or more zeros may be expressed in text by combining figures and words. The most important point is ease of reading the number.
   3,999,999
   four million
   9 million to 1 billion
   3.25 million or 3 $\frac{1}{4}$ million

Roman Numerals

It is generally preferable to use Arabic numbers in business correspondence since they are more easily understood than Roman numerals.

If you do need to use Roman numerals, follow these tips as well as the chart below to select the numerals.

■ A repeated letter repeats its value: II equals two (I equals one)

■ A letter placed after one of greater value adds to it: VI equals six (V equals five and I equals one)

■ A letter placed before one of greater value subtracts from it: IX equals nine (I equals one and X equals ten)

■ A line over a letter denotes multiplied by 1,000: $\overline{V}$ equals five thousand (V equals five and the line above means × 1,000)

Numbers

I	1	XL	40	C	100
II	2	XLV	45	CL	150
III	3	XLIX	49	CC	200
IV	4	L	50	CCC	300
V	5	LV	55	CD	400
VI	6	LIX	59	D	500
VII	7	LX	60	DC	600
VIII	8	LXV	65	DCC	700
IX	9	LXIX	69	DCCC	800
X	10	LXX	70	CM	900
XV	15	LXXV	75	M	1,000
XIX	19	LXXIX	79	MD	1,500
XX	20	LXXX	80	MM	2,000
XXV	25	LXXXV	85	MMM	3,000
XXIX	29	LXXXIX	89	MMMM or	
				MV	4,000
XXX	30	XC	90	$\overline{V}$	5,000
XXXV	35	XCV	95	$\overline{C}$	100,000
XXXIX	39	XCIX	99	$\overline{M}$	1,000,000

Dates

MDC	1600	MCML	1950
MDCC	1700	MCMLX	1960
MDCCC	1800	MCMLXX	1970
MCM or MDCCC	1900	MCMLXXX	1980
MCMX	1910	MCMXX	1990
MCMXX	1920	MM	2000
MCMXXX	1930	MMX	2010
MCMXL	1940	MMXX	2020

Chapter 4

Electronic Correspondence

Correspondence by electronic means is quickly outdating standard paper correspondence. Although it may be easy to be informal when communicating by fax or e-mail, you must keep in mind that these are both forms of business correspondence. Detailed below are general guidelines for writing, sending, and communicating business information by fax and e-mail.

Faxes

Faxing, transmitting a facsimile of a letter or memorandum over a telephone line, has become a popular method of business communication. The correspondence itself is usually preceded by a cover sheet, which contains relevant information on the sender, subject, and receiver of the fax. Most often the fax message itself will take the form of a memorandum, but resumes, news releases, and business forms may also be faxed.

Faxing is especially appropriate when time is a critical factor. It is a useful means of communication for ordering merchandise, confirming an appointment, or acknowledging receipt of a bill or shipment. A fax can be less appropriate for some correspondence. A personal letter of condolence should not be faxed. A formal invitation or letter of appreciation should also be mailed.

Fax Cover Sheet

A cover may precede the fax message. Many different fax covers are available, and your company may have a fax sheet with its name, logo, phone number, and other information printed on it. The cover may be programmed in the computer or fax machine, and the sender merely types the message. The fax cover should include the receiver's name, the receiver's department and company, the receiver's fax number, the sender's name and company, the number of pages transmitted, and the date and time. Additionally, the sender may wish to communicate his or her own telephone number and return address. The fax cover may follow the form of a memorandum:

TO: Lynne Golpher

                       Comptroller's Office

                       Grossman & Gladstein

FROM: Andy Fine

FAX NUMBER: (000) 111-2222

RE: Board Meeting Agenda

DATE: 4/5/02

TIME: 2:15 PM

PAGES: 3

If you do not receive all pages, please call (000) 111-2222.

E-mail

E-mail is a common means of communication. An e-mail is data or a message transmitted instantly from computer to computer through a modem that connects it to a telephone line. As is true of the fax, certain messages, such as formal invitations, should not be sent by e-mail. E-mail is an excellent means to communicate when time is of the essence. It is particularly suitable to confirm or arrange an appointment, acknowledge receipt of a shipment or payment, or send a personal message. A file may be attached to the e-mail for downloading. This attachment may contain an order form, a business report, or other important documents. A formal e-mail, one that is distributed to many persons, may follow memorandum form.

An e-mail closing may include the name, address, and phone and fax numbers of the sender.

Informal

Bob,

My business trip to Missouri tomorrow has been canceled. The weather looks good. How about a round of golf at Rolling Hills at 2:00?

Bill

Formal

TO: District Sales Representatives
RE: Sales Projections
DATE: March 1, 2002

The Board of Directors is reviewing company operations prior to implementing a reorganization plan. We would appreciate receiving your regional sales projections for the 2002–03 fiscal year by April 1.

Glenda Horton, Treasurer
Mars Electronics
100 Hillel Blvd.
Los Angeles, CA 00000
Ph: 000.111.2222
Fax: 000.111.2222

Chapter 5

The Memorandum

The memorandum, or memo, is used for written communications between offices or departments. Memos range from formal to informal, from one or two sentences to many pages. A memo may be a handwritten note to an employee confirming a meeting, a congratulatory notice to the company softball team, or a detailed explanation of a company policy. It may be mailed, faxed, or e-mailed.

Generally, memos tend to be short and topical. They deal with routine company matters, serving as written reminders or announcements of important policies, events, and procedures. Memos are often used to confirm information that has been discussed in conversation, record telephone messages, make requests, commend employees, report information, or to transmit documents. Some firms use preprinted memo forms for routine correspondence outside the company. For example, to order supplies or confirm a delivery date. Faxed communications frequently take the form of memos.

A memo, like all business correspondence, should be clear and concise. Make sure that the memo includes all relevant information, such as time, place, date, and order number. It is not necessary to add introductory or concluding remarks as in a business letter.

On some occasions, even for correspondence within an office, a letter may be more appropriate than a memo. A memo announcing the winner of a regional sales competition is appropriate, but the employee should also be sent a personal letter of congratulations. Serious criticisms or censure of an employee should always come in a private letter and not in a public memo. A memo becomes part of the company's public record. Any information of a private nature should be communicated through a phone call or personal meeting.

The Memorandum Form

Most firms use a standard form—either an off-the-shelf preprinted form or a company-designed form that may be programmed in a computer. This form may have preprinted lines or blank spaces after the guide words TO, FROM, DATE, and SUBJECT. Some firms use company letterhead stationery, sometimes on lesser-quality paper. For short communications, the form is often note-sized (8" × 5" or 4" × 5"). If your employer uses letterhead stationery for internal correspondence, then you will need to type in the title MEMORANDUM and the guide words.

Parts of the Memorandum

Title

Indicate on the letterhead stationery that the correspondence is a memo by typing "Memorandum" flush on the left margin or centered three or more spaces beneath the letterhead. This title may also appear in capitals and it may be underlined for emphasis:

WEINBERG WATER RESOURCES
119 Stang Street
Greensboro, NC 00000

MEMORANDUM

WEINBERG WATER RESOURCES
119 Stang Street
Greensboro, NC 00000

<u>MEMORANDUM</u>

To be less formal, you may use such titles as FROM THE DESK OF or INTEROFFICE MESSAGE in place of MEMORANDUM.

Receiver's Name

The receiver's name appears on the first line after the guide word *to*, and the salutation is omitted. Name alone is often sufficient, but especially in larger organizations, title and department or division may be included. Sometimes an address is helpful. Several forms, in either upper or lower case, are acceptable:

> To: Maya Benjamim

> To: Maya Benjamin, Director

> To: Maya Benjamin, Director of Play Therapy

> To: MAYA BENAMIN, DIRECTOR

> PLAY THERAPY, 119 A WING

Frequently, memos are addressed to a group of employees, a department, or a division:

> To: Patients Account Staff

> TO: ALL EMPLOYEES

Sender's Name

The sender's name appears on the second line under the guide word *from*. Sometimes the sender will also be identified by title, position, or department, especially if the memo is a policy statement. To emphasize that the memo represents the company's views, not just those of the person sending it, the writer may omit his or her personal name and use only the division or department. Several styles are acceptable:

> FROM: HOWARD STANG

> From: Howard Stang, Director of Admissions

> From: Director of Admissions

> FROM THE DIRECTOR OF ADMISSIONS

Date

The date is usually placed flush on the left margin under either *from* or *subject*. Three forms are acceptable for indicating the date of the memorandum:

traditional	month day, year
	August 19, 2002
government, science	day month year
military	19 August 2002
informal, handwritten	month/day/year
	8/19/02
European informal	day/month/year
	19/8/02

If time is of critical importance, then the time of day may also appear on this line.

Subject Line

The subject line should make clear the purpose of the memo. The title or brief statement of the message's content should be as short and precise as possible. A glance at the subject line should instantly tell the person receiving the memo what it concerns. The subject line will also facilitate filing the memo or placing the information on a calendar.

Avoid general titles, such as "claims" or "employee relations." State the specific issue under consideration, such as "health-insurance claims" or "new grievance guidelines."

The subject line is frequently capitalized. The Latin word *Re*, meaning "thing," may be used in place of "Subject":

SUBJECT: PARKING LOT ASSIGNMENTS

SUBJECT: Parking lot assignments

Subject: Parking lot assignments

RE: PARKING LOT ASSIGNMENTS

Re: Parking lot assignments

Brief memos with messages of temporary interest, such as report of a telephone call, may not include a subject line. For example, a short memo advising the recipient of a personal message from a spouse or confirming a doctor's appointment does not need a subject line.

Message Form

Most employers prefer the left-margin block style for a memo, but indented form may also be used. Check with your company to find the preferred style or use the preprinted or programmed forms, if available. While guidelines (TO, FROM, and so on) are usually double-spaced, the message itself is single-spaced, with double-spacing between paragraphs.

Signature

Most memos are not signed, but the reader may place initials after his or her name in the FROM line. In longer or more formal memorandums, the FROM line is sometimes omitted, and the sender's identity (signature over typed name and position) is placed at the end of the message.

Typist's Initials

Usually the initials of the typist are not included, but in longer memos they may be typed two spaces after the end of the message in the same form as in a letter.

Enclosures and Copies

Copies and enclosures are included as end notes in the same form as they are in a letter (see letter form, pages 12-13). Instead of listing copies, you may be asked to use preprinted forms, which include ROUTING or a list of names. (E-mail contains a "CC:" box for transmitting copies.) Each reader will sign his or her initials to acknowledge having read the memo and then pass it on to another person on the list.

Memorandum Typing Instructions

Letterhead

(3 spaces or more)

Memorandum (centering and underlining optional)

(2 spaces)

TO: Name (title, division, or department optional)

(2 spaces)

FROM: Name (initials or signature optional)

(2 spaces)

DATE: Month day, year (time and placement optional)

(2 spaces)

SUBJECT (or RE): Brief title or statement of contents

(2 spaces or more)

The message itself is single-spaced. Most firms prefer block style, but indented style may also be acceptable.

Double space between paragraphs. Keep paragraphs short.

(2 spaces)

(signature or typed name and title optional)

Typist's initials (optional)   (2 spaces)

Enclosures (optional)   (2 spaces)

Copies (optional)   (2 spaces)

Sample Memorandums

Commendation or Congratulations Memo

FROM THE DESK OF TOBY TALCHANA

TO: Ibrahim Saaed   DATE: May 27, 2002

On behalf of Hill Electronics, I want to offer my congratulations on your election to the editorial board of *Merchandising Today*. You've have had a commendable record in the consumer electronics industry, and we are proud to see you recognized. We appreciate all that you've done for the industry, and we look forward to working with you in the future.

Company Policy Memo

KEEVER PUBLISHING
12 Chippewa Drive
Durham, NH 00000
000.111.2222

MEMORANDUM

TO: All full-time, salaried employees

FROM: Arthur Huang, President

SUBJECT: New health insurance coverage

DATE: February 2, 2002

The Board of Directors of Keever Publishing is pleased to announce that a new health insurance policy offering comprehensive coverage for all full-time, salaried employees and their immediate families will go into effect on April 1.

TransAmerica Health will underwrite this much-improved policy. Representatives from TransAmerica will visit us on March 12 to explain the coverage and to enroll employees and their families.

I am pleased that the board has agreed to contract with TranAmerica. At a time of rising health care costs, we believe that this policy will ensure the economic viability of our company while giving our employees and their families the best protection possible.

(signature)

Company Policy Change Memo

TRISTATE FINANCIAL SERVICES
Suite 17, Franklin Plaza, Elkin, OH 00000
Tel: 000-111-2222 Web site: www.tfs.net

MEMORANDUM

To: Sales Staff

From: Evette Baumann

Date: March 6, 2002

Re: PARKING FOR PERSONAL VEHICLES

As you know, construction of the new sales office is scheduled to begin this spring. During construction we will not be able to use our west parking lot. We have arranged to lease parking space for company vehicles at the Inbal Company across the street. Beginning March 15, those of you who drive to work will have to make other arrangements for parking your personal vehicles.

Limited on-street parking is available on Asher Street, or you may wish to use the municipal lot at Town Centre and walk three blocks to the office. We will arrange morning and evening shuttle service from the office to this lot.

I apologize for the inconvenience, but I am sure that you will agree that the long-term benefits of the new facilities will greatly outweigh any temporary problems. When the construction is completed, we'll have a nicely landscaped parking lot with bright lighting and an assigned space for each staff member.

cc: Melinda Krehbiel   Mae Svensen
               Pat Suzuki   Briana Summerfeld
               Svan Chilkuri   Greg Pappas
               Deena Parisi   Bill Chen
               Sidney Davis   Maria Lopez

Inquiry Memo

INTEROFFICE MESSAGE

TO: Micah Lynn, Inventory

FROM: Janette Steele, Payroll

RE: Back order PY-77-71

DATE: 28 August 2002

On August 20, I asked the supply department to deliver three boxes of RW-CDs (10 per box), inventory number C-14. I received a notice from you on August 21 that you were out of stock but delivery was expected from OfficeMart on August 23.

Have you received this shipment? We urgently need the disks. If we do not have them in-house, then I will need to make arrangements for a purchase order so that I can buy them from a local retail store. Please call me at extension 91.

Report Memo (formal)

CITY OF GREENFIELD
TOWN HALL
P.O. BOX 112, GREENFIELD, TN 00000

MEMORANDUM

TO: Members of the Appearance Commission
FROM: Department of City Planning
DATE: 12 March 2002

RE: Guidebook on the Greenfield Sign Ordinance

The Appearance Commission has asked this office for suggestions on improving enforcement of the Greenfield Sign Ordinance, enacted by the Town Council on 14 December 2001.

Problem: The Appearance Commission is charged with protecting the character of Greenfield as a historic village. The commission has attempted to balance the need for retail businesses to advertise their services and products with the concern of local residents that Greenfield protect its traditional character. Greenfield's special ambiance as a historic village makes the town a pleasant place to live and draws tourists to the area. The newly enacted Sign Ordinance attempts to regulate the appearance of commercial signs in the village by setting guidelines for new signs and calling for the removal or renovation of some existing signs. The commission is concerned about enforcing this ordinance fairly and impartially. Several businesses have already complained to the commissioners and Town Council about the potential adverse effects of the ordinance.

Areas of Concern: On 8 March, the Appearance Commission met with an ad hoc committee of the Chamber of Commerce. Several areas of concern in interpreting and enforcing the new ordinance were defined:

*   Size of sign
*   Location
*   Materials

- Colors
- Lighting
- Three-dimensional figures and graphics
- Coordination of size and design with architecture
- Logos and franchise signs

Recommendations: The Appearance Commission recommends the publication by 1 August 2002 of a commercial sign guidebook listing specific criteria for designing new signs and renovating existing ones.

On April 23, the commission will hold a public meeting to explain the ordinance and to hear public opinion. Representatives of the business community, such as the Chamber of Commerce and citizen groups, such as the Greenfield Preservation Society, will be invited to participate.

Based on public comment, the commission will pass its recommendations to the Town Council dealing with aspects of the Sign Ordinance that are ambiguous or subject to interpretation. There is presently no regulation, for example, of portable signs. Other signs that do not conform may be deemed to have historic worth by virtue of their longevity or aesthetic merit. Drafting a guidebook should help the commissioners formulate policy that will cover such cases.

After the April hearings, the commission will draw a list of recommendations. A draft of a commercial sign guidebook will be submitted to the Town Council, local businesses, and community groups for their comments. At this point, the Town Council may wish to add amendments to the Sign Ordinance to correct any ambiguities or omissions. A revised handbook will then be published.

This office will be glad to meet with the Appearance Commission at any time to begin the process of drafting a commercial sign guidebook. We are prepared to offer legal and professional counsel as well as secretarial assistance.

Joel Samuelson
Director, Department of City Planning

Report Memo (informal)

RANCHERO ESTATES

12 Hacienda Trail,   Los Alamos, NM 00000

MEMORANDUM

To: Sales Agents

From: Frank Gonzalez, President

Date: 2 March 2002

Subject: February Housing Sales UP!

The numbers are in for housing sales in February, and the market looks to be strengthening. We sold 121 units, a 20 percent increase from last month and 33 percent higher than the figures for February 2001. Much of the improvement comes from new people moving into the area for the Formax Corporation plant, which will begin production on 15 March. Interest rates in February remained at just above 7 percent, which also helped spur sales. The prospect is for these rates to climb gradually in the coming months, so agents may wish to stress to customers the advantages of making their purchases now and locking in a low rate. At the staff meeting on 10 March, we will present a more complete report on sales, but the preliminary data suggest that the market is still strongest for starter homes under $200,000 and weakest at price levels above $450,000.

Scheduling Memo (meetings)

TO: STUDENT AFFAIRS STAFF

FROM: JAREEKA BARNETT

SUBJECT: JULY STAFF MEETING

Please mark your calendars and plan to attend the monthly staff meeting, Monday, July 24, at 3:00 in the conference room, 103 Peabody Hall. If you cannot attend, please leave a message at my e-mail address, Jareeka@edu.org.

Transmittal Memo (documents)

MEMORANDUM

TO:	Tanya Potter
	Ramiah Sarik
	Yutonya Gorton
	Emily Ann Fucello
FROM:	Laura Holly
DATE:	March 15, 2002
RE:	FISCAL 2001 OPERATIONS ENERGY AUDIT

Hiller and Levin have completed their energy audit of our Westmount plant. I am sending a copy of their report with this memo. It is the most comprehensive analysis that I have seen to date of the plant's operations. I call special attention to their recommendations.

Please read the report closely, and let me know as soon as possible what steps that you think that we should take to improve operating efficiency. Please send me your recommendations prior to our meeting. Once we achieve a consensus on a plan of action, we should arrange a meeting with senior management.

Memorandum Checklist

- ❑ Title (Memorandum or Interoffice Message)

- ❑ To

- ❑ From

- ❑ Date (placement optional)

- ❑ Subject or Re:

- ❑ Message

- ❑ Signature or initials (optional)

- ❑ Typist's initials (optional)

- ❑ Enclosures (optional)

- ❑ Copies or routing (optional)

Chapter 6

Meeting Minutes

Minutes are a written record of the transactions and recommendations of a meeting. Usually a secretary or committee member records them. The minutes are filed as a permanent record of the meeting. Copies are passed to the participants and other interested parties prior to their next meeting. Minutes must be clear, precise, and accurate.

When taking minutes, be sure to bring sufficient pens and note-taking paper, or you may type the proceedings on a notebook computer. Your company may also want you to record the meeting with dictation equipment. The minutes should contain only major topics and recommendations, not every point that is discussed. Since some speakers may not stick to the subject, you may have to reorganize the material when preparing the minutes. Keep your handwritten notes on file for verification. The typed minutes are an orderly and condensed version of the meeting. The tone should be formal and objective, reporting the major points and the names of the persons making them.

After the minutes are completed, they are usually first passed to the chairman or president for approval and then circulated to the participants as well as to absent members. The minutes should be submitted as soon as possible and distributed prior to the next meeting of the group. At the next meeting, each member will have a copy of the minutes; as a first order of business, the minutes may be amended or corrected, and approved by vote. The secretary then signs the minutes with the notation *approved.*

Each organization follows a house style in minutes. Informal minutes may be a simple chronological summary of what transpired in the meeting. For legal or organizational reasons, the minutes may be typed as a formal report, reflecting the agenda of the meeting. Most important, the minutes should follow a uniform format meeting after meeting.

Parts of Minutes

Title

Several styles are acceptable. A topic heading is direct and easy to read. Type "Minutes" either at the left margin or center of the page. The name of the committee or organization, the type of meeting, date, and place may follow it:

Minutes: Wordsworth Literary Society, Monthly Meeting, November 23, 2002

Or you may begin with a complete sentence conveying information as to the reason for the meeting, the name of the group, the date, and place of the meeting:

The annual meeting of the Friends of Northwood Hospice was held on August 3, 2002, in the boardroom of Riverdale Hospital, Farmingdale, NY.

Attendance

The minutes list the names of those who attend the meeting beginning with the presiding officer. To follow are several models:

Present: Sol Terry Reaper, chair; Lucinda McAdams, Julie Mendoza, Su Ling, and Angela Suarez

Attending: Stav Roer (presiding), Tamara Carpenter, Bill Lambeer, Ivan Smirnov

Chairperson Lillian Goldblum presided with forty-two members in attendance.

President Steven Valente welcomed ninety-seven delegates to the plenary session.

Approval of Minutes

A short statement makes note of any corrections or amendments to the reading of the minutes of the previous meeting. It names the person making the motion for approval of the minutes:

> Philip Stetson moved that the minutes be approved. The motion was seconded and carried.

Report

The text can take several forms. Informal minutes just summarize chronologically the major points discussed at the meeting. Formal minutes break down the discussion into subtopics based on the meeting's agenda, oral reports, or subjects discussed. The headings, placed against the left margin, may be underlined, boldfaced, or italicized for emphasis:

Treasurer's Report

<u>Treasurer's Report</u>

Treasurer's Report

After all agenda matters have been covered and all reports presented, space will be reserved for unfinished business or new business.

Date of Next Meeting

A statement of the time and place of the next meeting may be placed at the end of the report or at the beginning, after the attendance. This information may be capitalized to capture the reader's attention:

> NEXT MEETING: 7:30 PM, JANUARY 4, 2003, AT THE BOARDROOM, VALLEY NATIONAL BANK, WAYNE, NJ

Sample Minutes

Informal Minutes

A monthly meeting of the Ditto Industries Employee Social Welfare Committee was held at 2:00, April 15, 2002, in Suite 15 of the administration building. Attending were Joe Ciao (chair), Ezell Jackson, Annie Brown, Malik Stapleton, and Regina Johnston.

The Committee agreed that we would once again hold a company fundraiser for the Fairview Children's Hospital. Ezell pointed out that last year's campaign, a sale of chocolate bars, was disappointing. He reported that we only raised $440 for the hospital on sales of $1,240, and less than half of the employees participated. Regina and Annie pointed out that selling chocolates might be a poor choice at a time when people seem so diet conscious. We decided to explore new possibilities. Some members suggested that we find a product that would have more sales appeal and would yield higher profits. Suggestions included stationery, coffee mugs, or t-shirts. Others spoke in support of holding a company fundraising event like a picnic or softball game. Annie and Malik agreed to study the alternatives and report back at the next meeting. Joe said he would compile a new list of fundraising captains in each department. He also suggested that we set a minimal fundraising goal of $1,000 this year.

The meeting adjourned at 2:50 PM.

THE NEXT MEETING WILL BE HELD 2:00 PM, MAY 14, IN SUITE 15, ADMINISTRATION BUILDING

Annie Brown, Secretary

Formal Minutes

Minutes: Pottstown Parks Citizen Advisory Committee, July 1, 2002, at Town Council Chambers

Present: Terri Malovich, chairperson; Francine Stella, secretary; Boyd Benson, Henry Krizek, Gregory Christakos, John Ocharenko, Janet Miller, Rudolph Perkins, Stanley Kowalski, Ryan Flaherty, Julian Cohen, and Steve Petrus. Also present was Bill Clay, assistant manger of the Pottstown Parks Department.

Approval of the Minutes

Upon reading of the June 3 minutes Boyd Benson observed that his name had been omitted from those in attendance. Steve Petrus noted that his name was spelled incorrectly. The minutes were so amended. Julia Cohen moved that the amended minutes be approved. The motion was seconded and carried unanimously.

Greenwood Park Expansion

Bill Clay of the Pottstown Parks Department reported that the Town Council had authorized the purchase of 42 acres to expand Greenwood Park. The Council wants the Citizens Advisory Committee to recommend possible uses for the land. The department defined several alternatives:

Natural environmental area
Recreational fields
Mixed use

Gregory Christakos spoke in favor of keeping the area natural, noting that the site includes extensive streams and woodlands, which would make it ideal for trails and rustic picnic areas. John Ocharenko pointed out that the town park system lacks undeveloped land where people can commune with nature. He also pointed out the need for environmental protection of areas that may be classified as wetlands. Francine

Stella noted that current recreational facilities are overtaxed, and the youth soccer league has had to turn down applicants because of the lack of playing fields. Chair Terri Malovich suggested the possibility of a mixed-use compromise and requested volunteers for a subcommittee to explore the issue. Francine Stella, John Ocharenko, Julian Cohen, and Janet Miller agreed to serve.

Pottstown Street Fair

Terri Malovich noted that the Pottstown Street Fair will be held on Saturday, June 1, and she recommended that the Citizens Advisory Committee again set up a booth. We will distribute literature, erect displays, and have volunteers available to answer questions. Boyd Benson moved that the chair be authorized to appropriate $50 for a street fair booth. The motion was seconded and carried without debate.

Unfinished Business

Ryan Flaherty stated that he has been trying to find new members to join the Committee, but he has nothing definite to report. Several people mentioned that they are interested but have not yet committed.

New Business

Steve Petrus reported that he has received numerous complaints that the $35 enrollment free for participation in the Pottstown summer softball league is excessive. He noted that the fee was especially hard for families with several members playing. Henry Krizek moved that we ask the Parks Department to send a representative to our August meeting to explain the rates. The motion was seconded and carried.

The meeting adjourned at 10:00 PM.

NEXT MEETING: 7:30 PM, AUGUST 2, 2002, AT THE TOWN COUNCIL CHAMBERS, MAIN STREET

Francine Stella
Secretary

Minutes Checklist

❑ Organization name

❑ Time, date, and place of meeting

❑ Attendees, beginning with chair

❑ Approval of past minutes

❑ Agenda topics or reports

❑ Unfinished business

❑ New business

❑ Adjournment time

❑ Date of next meeting (placement optional)

❑ Approval and secretary's signature

Chapter 7

Business Reports

Business reports have two basic purposes:

1. To collect and interpret data so that an executive can make an informed decision;

2. To communicate information to staff, stockholders, customers, or other concerned parties.

The business report represents the best efforts of a company and its appearance should reflect that fact.

Formal and Informal Reports

Formal reports are usually sent to customers or stockholders. They are bound with printed covers and attractively formatted. The report is supported by tables and charts. Informal reports are usually circulated to staff members within a company. The pages may be stapled or paper-clipped together in the upper left-hand corner. Before preparing a report, check with an executive to determine your company's house style.

The next section will give you an understanding of the placement and purpose of the components of a business report. Note that a sample report is included at the end of this chapter to give you a visual of a business report layout.

Parts of the Business Report
Cover

The cover should be attractive as well as protective. A formal report cover may be glossy and include an illustration or company logo as well as the title. A cover for an informal report may consist of a typed page with the title printed in capital letters. A subtitle may be added after the title in one of two ways: put a colon after the title and type the subtitle in capitals, or type the subtitle in lower case under the title as follows:

THE 2003 CELL PHONE MARKET
Sales Prospects for Gemco

THE 2003 CELL PHONE MARKET: SALES PROSPECTS FOR GEMCO

Flyleaf (formal report only)

Insert a blank page after the cover.

Title Fly (formal report only)

Type the report title in capitals on the upper third of the page as it appears on the cover.

Title Page

The title page may serve as the cover of a report, especially if it is an informal report. The title page consists of several blocks: the title in capitals on the upper third of the page; the writer's name, title, department or address; the reader's name, title, and address; and the date of completion. Usually, these elements are centered on the page with spaces between the blocks. Many styles are acceptable, as long as the title page looks balanced and attractive. For informal or staff reports, the information may be briefer.

Letter of Authorization

A business report is often written in response to an order or a request for information from a person or a company. Include a copy of the letter that authorizes the report.

Letter of Transmittal

This letter serves as a foreword to the report. It states the purpose of the report, the research methods, the limitations of the project, and the possibilities for the future. The letter ends with a note of thanks and willingness to be of further help. The tone is positive and friendly. The letter of transmittal is typed on the letterhead stationery of the author of the report, who also signs it.

Acknowledgements (optional)

If others contributed to the preparation of the report, then the author may wish to add a page acknowledging their help. The writer may add his or her initials or name.

> The author wishes to thank the employees of McComber Graphics for their cooperation in preparing this report.
>
> Michiko Honda
>
> Special thanks to Ms. Jeanette Lupi, who offered valuable assistance as a researcher, and to Ms. Harriet Podsnap, who edited the manuscript.
>
> M.H.

Table of Contents

The table of contents guides the reader to specific topics in the report. It also serves as a brief outline of the report's contents and organization. The Table of Contents lists major topics and subtopics and page numbers. The contents page is often done last because it contains a complete listing of all material in the report. A Table of Contents should look well organized.

Type TABLE OF CONTENTS or CONTENTS in capitals, centered, at the top of the page:

TABLE OF CONTENTS

CONTENTS

Topic headings appear in capitals on the left margin. Subtopics are indented at least three spaces. Double-space before and after headings, but single-space between subtopic headings. If the report uses Roman numerals before topic headings and capital letters before subtopic headings, as in an outline, then the Table of Contents should do the same.

To separate the topic and subtopic headings from the page numbers, use periods, dashes, or blank spaces. The first page of the section is listed on the right margin. Several styles are acceptable:

I. REGIONAL SALES MARKETS 1

   A.   Eastern Zone 3

   B.   Western Zone 8

REGIONAL SALES MARKETS   1

   Eastern Zone   3

   Western Zone   8

List of Illustrations (optional)

If the report contains more than three charts, graphs, pictures, maps, or tables of statistics, then compile a List of Illustrations. If only one or two illustrations are included, then the list may be included in the Table of Contents. The form of the List of Illustrations should be the same as the Table of Contents. Type LIST OF ILLUSTRATIONS or ILLUSTRATIONS in capitals at the top center of the page.

ILLUSTRATIONS

LIST OF ILLUSTRATIONS

Assign a letter or number to each illustration as a guide to the reader. The letter or number appears on the left-hand margin. The title of the illustration is typed in capitals. The page number is typed on the right-hand margin. Several styles are acceptable:

Table	Title	Page
I.	PHOTO OF PLANT SITE	17
II.	CONSTRUCTION COSTS	42
III.	STATISTICAL ABSTRACT	53

Table		
A.	PHOTO OF PLANT SITE	17
B.	CONSTRUCTION COSTS	42
C.	STATISTICAL ABSTRACT	53

Abstract (optional)

An abstract, also called a summary, synopsis, digest, or précis, is a brief review of the whole report. A busy executive may want to read quickly the major points or the recommendations of the report without studying the text in depth. If the letter of transmittal summarizes the major findings of the report, then the abstract may be omitted. The abstract should not be longer than one page.

Text

The text consists of an introduction, body, and conclusion. The report may be typed in paragraph form without breaks, or it may be divided into topics and subtopics with headings at the beginning of each section.

Headings

Headings make a business report easier to read by highlighting the organization. The headings should be coordinated with the listings in the Table of Contents.

Some styles place the headings flush on the left margin. Others center major and minor topic headings. Two blank lines separate the title and major and minor topic headings. Paragraph headings are usually underlined and indented five spaces and run into the text of the paragraph. Major topics are usually typed in capitals while minor topics are printed in lower case and underlined.

Outline form, based on the table of contents, may be used in the text:

I. MAJOR TOPIC

A. <u>Minor Topic</u>

      1. Subtopic

          a. <u>Paragraph Heading</u>

Or, if the outline form is not used, the headings may simply be typed without numbers or letters. To follow are two styles:

MAJOR TOPIC

<u>Minor Topic</u>

Subtopic

      <u>Paragraph Heading</u>

MAJOR TOPIC

<u>Minor Topic</u>

Subtopic

      <u>Paragraph Heading</u>

I. MARKETING STRATEGIES FOR 2003

A. <u>Advertising Opportunities</u>

      1. Television Campaigns

MARKETING STRATEGIES FOR 2003

<u>Advertising Opportunities</u>

Television Campaigns

Introduction

The introduction usually contains a brief history of the company and provides background for the report. It also includes a statement of purpose, which may include information on who authorized the report and why it was requested. In the introduction, the writer seeks to justify the need for the report, documenting the problem and suggesting the means by which it can be corrected. The writer of the report also describes research methods, where and how information was obtained, and the limits of the assignment.

Body

The body of the report contains a discussion of the problem. It should be objective and balanced. Do not confine the discussion exclusively to support your recommendation, but give consideration to other alternatives including those that you do not recommend. Charts or tables of statistics may appear within the report to support the conclusion.

The discussion will vary with the specific subject. Try to organize the discussion by breaking it down into topics and subtopics. Most topics can be classified by alternatives, criteria, or similar categories. For example, a study of sites for a new business may be broken down into subtopics by criteria—retail market, population, construction costs—or by alternatives, such as Chicago, New York, or Los Angeles.

Conclusion

Conclusions or recommendations are usually found at the end of the report to give a sense that they are the final result of a well-built case. Conclusions or recommendations may also be stated at the very beginning of the report.

This section states succinctly the most convincing reasons for recommending the choice of action. If several alternatives have been considered, then do not neglect to point out their advantages or disadvantages. For emphasis, state the recommendation in either the opening or closing sentence of this section.

Tables

Statistics and data in the text of a report can be confusing. For this reason, data may be presented in the form of tables, charts, or graphs. This information can be presented within the text or in an Appendix at the end. If the data is presented in the text, then it should be highlighted by a box, blank space, or a separate page.

Population of Potential Market Sites, 2003	
Cape Aaron	123,776
Johnstown	127,998
Lilahville	145,889

If the tables are included in the Appendix, then you may refer the reader to the specific exhibit with a note in the text.

After five years, the cost savings of renting over building will be under $2,000, as Appendix C illustrates.

After five years, the cost savings of renting over building will be under $2,000. (See Appendix C.)

Footnotes (optional)

Footnotes indicate sources of information that are used in a report. Footnotes are used when words are quoted directly or ideas are borrowed in paraphrase. Less often, a footnote reports secondary information that the writer does not wish to include in the text. Do not clutter the text with footnotes.

A footnote is indicated by a number that appears at the end of the borrowed material. It is typed without a space, one third above the line. The footnote number should appear outside quotation marks:

George Fox in his annual economic forecast predicts "modest levels of growth with minimal inflationary pressures."[1]

Market trends, according to a report in *Sales Today*, will continue downward for the next three to five years.[2]

Footnotes are usually numbered consecutively (1,2,3,4....) throughout a report. Other styles start over again with the beginning of each page or chapter. The footnote may be typed on the bottom of the page and separated from the text by a line twenty spaces long that is typed from the left margin. More often, footnotes appear on a separate page at the end of the text marked NOTES or FOOTNOTES. For footnote style and placement, check the style sheet or manual preferred by your company.

Footnotes follow a basic form:

Books

Author's Name, *Book Title* (Place of Publication: Publisher, Date), p. #.

Magazines

Author's Name, "Title of Article," *Magazine*, # (Date), pp. #.

The footnote itself is usually indented six to seven spaces from the left margin. Some styles start the footnote flush on the left margin. First, type the footnote number. It may be raised one third above the line or typed directly on the line. If the number is typed on the line, then a period after the number is optional. Next, leave a space. The second line is typed flush with the number. Several forms are acceptable, but be consistent. Use one form only throughout your report.

book author	1 Luis Sandoval, *The International Coal Trade* (New York: Moby Press, 1999), p. 18.
multiple authors	2 Frank Li and Yvette Lim, *Marketing Today* (Boston: Tharp Press, 2001), p. 213.
no author stated	3 "Grain Futures," *Food Industry Review*, XXI:17(April, 2002), 312.
article from magazine	4 Thomas Kucinski, "The Federal Reserve Board and Money Supply," *Financial News*, 18 (May 27, 2002), 15.
unpublished	5 Terry Soter, personal letter of December 27, 2001.
	6 Anthony Pirelli, telephone interview, February 2, 2002.

Subsequent references to the same source do not have to copy the complete footnote. Instead, the author and page number will suffice:

7 Kucinski, p. 18.

If more than one book by the same author is footnoted, then add the title in the subsequent references:

8 Sandoval, *The International Coal Trade*, p. 221.

Appendix (optional)

An Appendix contains background information that is not included in the body of the report. This includes graphs, charts, illustrations, and documents. A separate sheet with the title "Appendix" typed in the center separates this section from the body of the report. You may also group the material into categories by typing a letter or number at the top of each page, such as Appendix A, Appendix B, and Appendix C; or Appendix 1, Appendix 2, and Appendix 3.

Bibliography (optional)

A bibliography is a list of all sources of information used to write the report, whether or not the sources appear in the footnotes. The bibliography appears on a separate sheet at the end of the report. The bibliography is compiled alphabetically beginning with the author's last name or, if no author is stated, with the title.

A bibliographic listing contains essentially the same information as the footnote but in somewhat different form. The last name of the author appears first. Periods rather than commas are used to separate elements. All the pages of an article are listed, not just the specific page reference. If the volume number is stated, then it is not necessary to type "pp." before the page numbers. Bibliographies follow a basic form:

book	Last name, First name. *Title.* City of publication: Publisher, Date.
article	Last name, First name. "Title." *Magazine*, vol.# (Date), pp.#.

To prepare a bibliography, type on the top of the page in capitals:

BIBLIOGRAPHY

Each reference is typed flush on the left margin. The second line is indented five to seven spaces. If the bibliography lists more than one work by a single author, then subsequent references begin with a six-space line followed by a period rather than the author's name.

Sharp, Rebecca. *Successful Salesmanship*. New York: Vanity Press, 1998.

_____. *Trends in Sales and Marketing Today*. New York: Vanity Press, 2001.

To follow are some sample bibliographic entries:

book	Heep, Uriah. *The International Textile Trade*. Boston: Berkeley Press, 1999.
multiple authors	Smallweed, Harold and Turlington, Esther. *New Approaches to Retail Sales*. Atlanta: Peachtree Publications, 2001.
no author stated	"Microprocessors of Tomorrow." *Computer Reports*. 11(May, 2002), 281-283.
article from a magazine	Kucinski, Bill. "The Federal Reserve Board and Money Supply." *Financial News*. 18 (August, 2001), 379-391.
unpublished material	Sirahata, Teri. Personal Letter, May 27, 2002. Valvano, Michael. Telephone Interview, June 6, 2001.

Typing Instructions for Reports

Margins

Left and right	$1\text{-}1\frac{1}{4}$ inches (unbound)
	$1\frac{1}{2}$ inches (bound)
Top	2 inches on first page
	1 inch on all other pages
Bottom	$1\text{-}1\frac{1}{2}$ inches

Paragraphs

Paragraphs should be indented at least three spaces. Do not begin a paragraph on the last line of a page or hyphenate the last word in a paragraph. If a paragraph is typed on more than one page, then make sure that the second page contains more than two lines of the paragraph.

Spacing

For ease of reading, business reports are usually double-spaced. Single-spacing is permissible but less preferable.

Quotes

Quoted or extracted material over three lines in length may be single-spaced and indented at least five spaces on the left and right margins:

> The sales director spoke directly to the executive committee on the need to improve sales performance:
>
> > Aggressive marketing can demonstrably raise sales. We tend to be a bit lax, believing that our reputation will sell the product. I'd like to see us advertise the quality edge of our merchandise.

He continued to outline the components of an advertising campaign that the company should implement.

Model Page for a Business Report

<u>TITLE</u>

(2 spaces)

MAJOR TOPIC _____

(2 spaces)

MINOR TOPIC

(2 spaces)
_____
(2 spaces)

Subtopic

(1 space)
_____
(2 spaces)

Paragraph Heading _____

Sample Report

SITE SELECTION FOR A NEW RIVERVIEW HEALTH CLUB

Prepared by
Maceo Davis
Archway Consultants
for
Anthony Pesci, President
Riverview Health Clubs
December 27, 2002

TABLE OF CONTENTS

RIVERVIEW HEALTH CLUBS

12 Apache Drive, Tuscon, Arizona 00000

000.111.2222 / www.riverview.com

March 17, 2002

Mr. Maceo Davis, Executive Director
Archway Consultants
78 Ridge Boulevard
Phoenix, AZ 00000

Dear Mr. Davis:

As I mentioned in our meeting of February 25, Riverview Health Clubs is interested in expanding. We would like you to survey three locations in Seneca, Walhalla, and Tougaloo and report to us on which site offers the best potential market.

Riverview currently operates three facilities in Arizona. Our clubs are designed for fitness and relaxation, and we offer facilities for our customers to work out on exercise machines, engage in weight training, and relax in our fitness centers. These centers contain saunas, whirlpools, and steam rooms.

We operate exercise clubs with the finest equipment and service. Our annual dues are $750, so we will need to expand into an area that is relatively affluent.

As noted in our conversation, we would appreciate your report by May 15 so that we can review it prior to our board meeting. Please call me if you need more information or if you wish access to our records or facilities.

Yours truly,

Anthony Pesci, President

AP/dg

ARCHWAY CONSULTANTS
78 Ridge Boulevard
Phoenix, AZ 00000
Ph: 000.111.2222
Fax: 000.111.2222
E-mail: archway@net.com

May 4, 2002

Mr. Anthony Pesci, President
Riverview Health Clubs
12 Apache Drive
Tuscon, Arizona 00000

Dear Mr. Pesci:

As you requested in your letter of March 17, I have reviewed the market for a new River Health Club facility and have examined three sites in Seneca, Walhalla, and Tougaloo. Archway Consultants recommends that your health and fitness center should be built at the shopping mall currently under construction in Tougaloo.

We reviewed the relative merits of each location relative to population, market characteristics, and facility costs. Seneca is the largest city, and Walhalla offers a stable business environment, but Tougaloo offers the best market for growth. As the mall in Tougaloo is now under construction, Riverview will be able to design a custom facility without large development and construction costs.

I will be glad to meet with you to explain further our reasons for recommending the Tougaloo site. Please feel free to call me at your convenience.

Cordially,
Maceo Davis
Executive Director

SUMMARY

This report examined locations in Seneca, Walhalla, and Tougaloo to determine the best location for a new branch of the Riverview Health Club. After examining population characteristics, income levels, and the retail markets, Archway Consultants concluded that Tougaloo, which is a rapidly growing university and research center, offered the best opportunity for a profitable operation.

INTRODUCTION

Riverview Health Clubs operates multipurpose fitness and recreational centers that appeal to an increasingly health-conscious population. Since opening its first club in Tucson in 1994, Riverview has expanded to locations in Phoenix (1997) and Flagstaff (1999). All three units have proven profitable with net sales of more than $6 million in the 2001 fiscal year. Membership has grown rapidly, and the centers now operate at nearly full capacity, averaging almost 600 members per location. Additional monies are derived from guest fees, special user charges, rentals, and retail equipment sales. With annual membership dues of $750, Riverview Health Club appeals to an affluent population.

<u>Statement of Purpose</u>

Mr. Anthony Pesci, President of Riverview Health Clubs, has authorized Archway Consultants to conduct a site survey to determine the best location for Riverview's expansion. The three alternatives are a converted warehouse in Seneca, a construction site in Walhalla, and a shopping mall in Tougaloo.

2

<u>Method</u>

Archway Consultants investigated each location by three criteria:

1. population

2. retail market

3. facilities

Each location was studied to determine income levels of the population and potential growth trends. Archway also interviewed local developers, retailers, and Chamber of Commerce officials to gain a sense of the business climate in each area.

Scope

This report confines its investigation to parameters defined by Riverview Health Clubs. Alternative construction sites are available at each location, but are not reviewed here. The criteria established were deemed to be the most applicable, but other factors such as the relative age of the population may also influence the choice of a location. [1]

POPULATION

Seneca

The largest of the three cities, Seneca has a population of 143,672. Since the 1980s, its population has been stable. The median income is a relatively high $39,567, but only a small percentage of its population (2.5) falls in the upper-income brackets.

3

Walhalla

The population has experienced steady growth, but the metropolitan population of 133,876 is significantly smaller than Seneca's. Of all three sites, Walhalla has the highest median income ($40,103) and a significant percentage of its population is affluent; 4.5 percent earn more than $50,000 annually.

Tougaloo

Though it currently has the smallest population, Tougaloo has experienced rapid growth in the past twenty years. The population has nearly doubled since 1980 and now totals 131,875. The median income of $39,350 is competitive with both Seneca and Walhalla. Almost 11 percent of its population is listed in the highest income bracket, reflecting the significant number of professionals who have moved to the area recently for the research park and state university complex.

Median Family Income, 2000

Seneca	$39,567
Walhalla	40,103
Tougaloo	39,360

Source: Statistical Abstract of the Southwest

4

RETAIL MARKET

Seneca

Retail sales have been in a prolonged slump, reflecting national economic trends. Ms. Felice Gonzalez, director of the Chamber of Commerce, described local business conditions as "generally flat."[2] The principal employer, Dedmon Industries, has been phasing out its operation and transferring its administrative personnel. Data indicate that a large percentage of disposable income is spent on the home, food, and transportation rather than on recreation or entertainment.

Walhalla

The economic situation is stable. Walhalla is a banking and financial center, and these institutions have proven to be secure, experiencing steady if limited growth.

Retail sales have remained level for several years despite the national downturn. The population is primarily white-collar workers, with a significant proportion at upper-income levels. Spending on recreation and entertainment is strong.

Tougaloo

Once an agricultural market town, Tougaloo has the makings of a "booming post-industrial center."[3] The state university campus established in 1965 has expanded rapidly to 18,500 students. A state-subsidized research park opened in 1981, which has succeeded in attracting a mix of electronic and pharmaceutical firms, including Fuchs Electronics, Weiner Computers, and Kilgore Chemicals. The university and research park are drawing to the area a large and well-paid professional population. Median income, though slightly below those of Seneca and Walhalla, is rising rapidly and this trend should continue. Data suggests that the Tougaloo population spends a large percentage of its disposable income on recreation and entertainment.

5

FACILITIES

Seneca

A refurbished warehouse is currently available on South Street, which is two blocks from the town center. The building offers nearly 15,000 square feet of floor space that is sufficient for offices, fitness center, and exercise and locker rooms. Rental should be approximately $18 per square foot or $270,000 annually. A two-year lease is available. The building requires major renovation. Another problem is the lack of parking space because only a nearby municipal lot, which charges one dollar per hour, could handle the expected flow of traffic. The downtown location would appeal strongly to office workers and commuters, but would be less attractive to suburbanites.

<u>Walhalla</u>

The site is currently an open lot located on Route 17, which is a major thoroughfare. The building can be designed to Riverview's specifications, but current construction costs of $110 per square foot require a large cash outlay. Conveniently located near an exit to the I-90 beltway, the site offers easy access to major subdivisions and retail and office complexes. It is situated on the town's north side, which is the area of greatest suburban growth.

<u>Tougaloo</u>

The site is in a major shopping mall now under construction. The building currently has 41,000 square feet of unrented space, and Mr. Sam Woodfin, sales agent for Bestworth Developers, has stated that he would work with Riverview in designing facilities. Rentals are $19 per square foot. The mall has already received commitment from a major luxury department story—Gladstein's—as well as several dry-good franchises that cater to an affluent clientele. The mall is located at the intersection of Interstate 15 and Route 301. A development of 300 luxury town houses is now under construction three miles from the mall.

6

RECOMMENDATIONS

Archway Consultants recommends that Riverview Health Club opens its new branch in Tougaloo. It best meets the requirements of population, site, and retail market.

<u>Seneca</u>

The city offers a large population base, but its economy is stagnant. Few data indicate that the trends will improve. The site is inconvenient to Riverview's consumer market and the facility has critical shortcomings, especially with parking. Rental and renovation costs are prohibitive.

<u>Walhalla</u>

This site is an attractive choice with a stable population and sound economic base. The area is currently the most affluent of the three alternatives. Developing the Walhalla site, however, will require substantial construction costs.

<u>Tougaloo</u>

Though the smallest in population, Tougaloo offers the greatest opportunity for growth. The trend indicates rapid expansion of the local economy with an affluent, active population. The mall site can be tailored to fit Riverview's needs at a minimal cost. For these reasons, Archway Consultants strongly recommends that the new Riverview Health Club be located in the Tougaloo mall.

7

NOTES

1 Archway Consultants recommends that Riverview should conduct a survey of its members to draw a more detailed statistical profile of its potential consumer market.

2 Felice Gonzalez, interview held at the Seneca Chamber of Commerce, March 23, 2001.

3 Thomas Hechinger, *Tougaloo: A City for Tomorrow*, (Phoenix: Arrowhead Press, 1999), p. 17.

8

APPENDIX

Population

	1980	1990	2000
Seneca	141,506	142,891	143,672
Walhalla	121,613	128,403	133,876
Tougaloo	91,312	113,645	131,598

Family Income by Percentage, 2000

	under 20,000	20,000-25,000	25,000-30,000	30,000-40,000	over 40,000
Seneca	29.6	15.9	14.0	28.0	12.5
Walhalla	20.6	15.6	15.1	33.6	15.5
Tougaloo	15.4	15.1	15.2	37.5	17.1

Distribution of Disposable Income by Percentage, 2000

	Food	Housing	Transport	Clothing	Medical	Recreation
Seneca	30.8	18.6	9.0	9.2	4.2	10.5
Walhalla	24.1	22.1	9.1	7.6	5.6	11.6
Tougaloo	20.4	22.5	8.0	7.4	3.9	14.7

Source: U.S. Census Bureau Statistics

9

BIBLIOGRAPHY

Banks, John. Editor. *Economic Survey of the Sunbelt*. Houston: Long-horn Publications, 1999.

Gonzalez, Felice. Interview. Seneca Chamber of Commerce, March 23, 2000.

Hechinger, Thomas. *Tougaloo: A Community for Tomorrow*. Phoenix: Arrowhead Press, 1999.

Huang, Lee. "Marketing Opportunities in Recreation." *Southwest Business Review*. 28 (April, 2001), 17-29.

Seneca Chamber of Commerce. *Economic Prospects for a New Millennium*. Seneca: Woodside Printers, 2000.

United States Bureau of the Census. *Statistical Abstract of the United States, 2000*. Washington: United States Government Printing Office, 2001.

Business Report Checklist

- ❏ Cover (optional)

- ❏ Flyleaf (optional)

- ❏ Title fly (optional)

- ❏ Title page

- ❏ Letter of authorization

- ❏ Letter of transmittal

- ❏ Acknowledgements (optional)

- ❏ Table of Contents

- ❏ List of Tables or Illustrations (optional)

- ❏ Abstract (summary or précis)

- ❏ Text

- ❏ Footnotes (optional)

- ❏ Appendix (optional)

- ❏ Bibliography (optional)

Chapter 8

News Releases

A firm seeks to promote its services or products through attention-getting news releases. A news release should describe an event of significance: a new product or service, opening a business, a merger, a new branch or location, major promotion, business expansion, reorganization, or new management. The release should be written in journalistic style. The information is presented from most important to least important, from main ideas to specific facts. It begins by answering who, what, when, where, why, and how.

The style and tone should be clear, vivid, and easy to read. Do not exaggerate the importance of the event through a hard sell or excessive superlatives. Photos may be appended by paper clip, not by glue or staples. A cover letter is not necessary. The data must be current. Remember, finally, that an editor may choose to print only part of your release, often only the first sentence. Make every word count.

Parts of a News Release
Title

Center NEWS RELEASE or PRESS RELEASE in capitals on the center of the page.

Heading

The news release begins with information for the newspaper editor. Two lines below the title type the heading flush with the left margin. The heading includes the name of the company, the contact person for the release, the contact person's e-mail address and telephone number, the company's address, and the release date. (FOR IMMEDIATE RELEASE or FOR RELEASE ON DECEMBER 27, 2002).

SHANDY KENNELS, INC.
contact: Gracie Crowther
telephone: 000-000-0000
e-mail: shandy_kennels@internet.com
118 Homer Road
Jaffa, KY 00000

FOR RELEASE ON FEBRUARY 2, 2002

Subject Line

The title states the company's business and the subject of the release. Typed in capitals, it is centered two lines below the heading.

GRAND OPENING OF SHANDY DOG

BOARDING KENNELS

Dateline

Two lines below the subject line, indent two spaces and enter the dateline, composed of the city (and, if necessary, the state) and the date in upper and lower case, followed by an em dash (long dash):

Jaffa, KY, February 2, 2002—

The text follows immediately after the dash.

Typing Instructions

The news release should be double-spaced with one-inch margins. Use $8\frac{1}{2}$" × 11" paper. If possible, the release should be limited to a single sheet. If more than one page is required, then center the word MORE in capitals at the bottom of the page and begin the next page flush on the margin with a one-word title and page number:

Kennels-2

At the end of the news release, center one of the following:

(END)

Sample News Release

NEWS RELEASE

COMET DRUGS
contact: Abdul Khalid
telephone: 000-000-0000
e-mail: comet@drug.net
123 Garner Lane
Hartford, CT 00000

FOR IMMEDIATE RELEASE

ARI BOYAN NEW PRESIDENT OF COMET DRUGS

Hartford, CT, April 24, 2002—Comet Drugs, the Hartford-based discount drugstore chain, has announced the appointment of Ari Boyan as president, effective May 1.

"Boyan brings to Comet Drugs broad experience as a retail manager with special expertise in the pharmaceutical field," stated Harold Kaplan, board chairman.

For the past seven years, Boyan has served as executive vice president of Z-Mart department stores where he was responsible for establishing full-service pharmacies in the national discount chain. Boyan, 43, holds a BS in pharmacology from the University of North Carolina and an MBA from Duke University.

"I remain committed to Comet's policy of offering high-quality generic products at competitive prices," Boyan stated at a press conference, announcing his appointment.

Since its founding in Hartford in 1978, Comet has grown rapidly to become one of New England's leading retail drugstore chains. It now operates 124 stores in a five-state area. Its gross sales were $359 million in 2002.

###

Chapter 9

Resumes

The resume is a personal data sheet that accompanies a letter of application for a job. The resume may be filed with a placement service or employment agency. It should be clean, orderly, and attractive as it represents the applicant's character and qualifications. Word processing and desktop publishing allow you to design a resume with a variety of fonts and layouts. You can tailor the contents for a specific position, emphasizing those aspects of your education or work experience that are most relevant. A good resume can win an applicant an interview that may lead to a job offer.

Resumes come in a variety of formats. Professional people often are asked to file a form called a vitae—a Latin word meaning "life"—when applying for grants or other technical work. The vitae includes sections on research and publication. Some resumes include past job descriptions that list duties and special skills. The two basic forms of the resume, however, are the chronological and the functional.

Chronological Resume

The chronological resume is organized by time. It presents general information, so it can be used for a variety of purposes, not just for a specific position. It is designed to present the applicant's background clearly and easily so that an employer can review quickly the person's qualifications. For this reason, try to fit your resume on one page. The chronological resume is especially appropriate for recent graduates or persons with minimal work experience.

Functional Resume

The functional resume is organized by categories that are relevant to a specific job. These categories may include career goals, work experience, or special skills. It highlights areas that appeal to a particular employer. Though done in outline form, the functional resume may use paragraph blocks. Under each section, phrases rather than sentences are acceptable.

Parts of the Resume

Personal Data

The resume, whether chronological or functional, should list your name, address, and telephone number at the top.

Tyrone Curtis Stephens
22 Elm Street
Houston, Texas 00000
(000) 111-2222
Tyrone@college.edu

Career Objective (optional)

A resume can state your ultimate goal or specific job interest in seeking employment. The chronological resume usually consists of a short general statement while the functional resume may be more descriptive.

(chronological)

CAREER GOAL   Retail sales management

(functional)

Career Objective

Seeking position as manager at a retail department store or franchise outlet. Special interest in athletic gear and sporting goods.

Education

List your educational record from present to past. You may also add your degrees, major areas of study, and special honors.

(chronological)

EDUCATION
1991–1992: B.S. Wayne State University
                Major: Business Administration
1990–1991: A.S. Vincennes Junior College
                Major: Business

(functional)

Educational Background in Business

Received Bachelor of Science from Wayne State University in 1992; majored in business administration with concentration in marketing and management. Received A.S. in 1991 from Vincennes Junior College in business with on-the-job training in retail sales.

Employment History

List your work experience beginning with your most recent job and going back to your graduation from high school or college. Again, several formats are acceptable. The information should reflect those qualifications that you wish to emphasize. In the chronological resume, give enough data so that the person reviewing your resume can locate your employers. Do not leave gaps in time.

(chronological)

WORK EXPERIENCE

1999–2002: Assistant Manager, Mercury Sporting Goods, Livonia, MI 00000
1998–1999: Sales Associate, Footfast Athletic Shoes, Vincennes, IN 00000
1995–1998: Salesman, Bullard Discount Sales, Gary, IN 00000

(functional)

Retail Sales Manager

Broad experience in retail sales both in customer service and management. Two years as Assistant Manager of Mercury Sporting Goods, Livonia, MI, with responsibility for scheduling, stocking, and accounting. Sales Associate at Footfast Athletic Shoes, Vincennes, IN, working in retail sales of shoe products. Salesman at Bullard Discount Sales, Gary, IN, responsible for sales and inventory.

Activities and Interests (optional)

This section should list activities, awards, interests, hobbies, or memberships that you believe would appeal to a prospective employer. If you are applying for a newspaper job, for example, then you might wish to list publications or writing talent.

(general)

Activities and Interests

Volunteer Work: YMCA basketball coach, Big Brother, Fellowship of Christian Athletes

Hobbies: track, basketball, photography

Honors: YMCA Coach of the Year; FCA, chapter president

(functional)

Community Service

Volunteered with youth sports team. Served as Big Brother to inner-city, grammar-school child. Volunteered as YMCA basketball coach and voted Coach of the Year. Elected president of collegiate Fellowship of Christian Athletes chapter.

References

Resumes frequently list references at the bottom of the page. This information may also be listed in a cover letter. You may merely state that references are available upon request. Be sure that you have the permission of your references before listing their names.

(general)

References

Peter Markowitz	Dr. Lynette Jones
Mercury Sporting Goods	School of Business
16 Van Alstyne Road	Wayne State University
Livonia, MI 00000	Detroit, MI 00000

References are available upon request.

Sample Chronological Resume

Tyrone Curtis Stephens
12 Elm Street
Houston, Texas 00000
(000) 111-2222
Tyrone@college.edu

EDUCATION	1992–1994:	B.S., Wayne State University, Detroit, MI Major: Business Administration
	1991–1992:	A.S., Vincennes Junior College, Vincennes, IN Major: Business
EMPLOYMENT	1995–2002:	Assistant Manager, Mercury Sporting Goods, Livonia, MI 00000
	1994–1995:	Sales Associate, Footfast Athletic Shoes, Vincennes, IN 00000
	1992–1994:	Salesman, Bullard Sales, Gary, IN
COMMUNITY SERVICE	1995–2002	YMCA Basketball Coach, Detroit, MI
	1992–1995	Big Brother volunteer, Gary, IN
	1991–1992	Fellowship of Christian Athletes

HONORS

Basketball scholarship, Vincennes Junior College

Coach of the Year, Detroit YMCA

Fellowship of Christian Athletes, chapter president

REFERENCES

Peter Markowitz	Dr. Lynette Jones
Mercury Sporting Goods	School of Business
16 Van Alstyne Road	Wayne State University
Livonia, MI 00000	Detroit, MI 00000

Sample Functional Resume

Tyrone Curtis Stephens
22 Elm Street
Houston, Texas 00000
(000) 111-2222
Tyrone@college.edu

Career My goal is to work for a firm specializing in retail.

Objectives Customer sales of sporting goods. I have experience and am seeking an entry-level managerial position in a franchise or department store.

Education Received a B.S. in business administration from Wayne State University in 1994 with a concentration in marketing and management. Earned an A.S. in business from Vincennes Junior College where I participated in a work-study program.

Retail Sales Experience Broad experience in retail sales both in customer service and management. Two years as Assistant Manager of Mercury Sporting Goods, Livonia, MI, with responsibility for scheduling, stocking, and accounting. Sales Associate at Footfast Vincennes, IN, working in retail sales of sports shoes products. Salesman at Bullard Discount Sales, Gary, IN, responsible for inventory control.

Community Service Have worked as a volunteer with youth sports team. Served as Big Brother to inner-city, grammar-school child. Volunteered as YMCA basketball coach, voted Coach of the Year. Elected president of collegiate Fellowship of Christian Athletes chapter.

References available upon request

Resume Checklist

❑ Personal data
  name
  address
  telephone number

❑ Career goal or job interest (optional)

❑ Education

❑ Employment history

❑ Activities and interests (optional)

❑ Special skills (optional)

❑ References

Chapter 10

Envelopes

Here are some general guidelines for preparing envelopes for business corre-spondence. Be sure to check if your company has a standard method for enve-lopes.

Addresses

Envelopes are addressed in block style. Businesses generally use envelopes with the company's name, address, and zip code preprinted in the upper left-hand corner. If the address is not preprinted or if the letter is personal, then type the sender's name and address in the upper left-hand corner. Your word-pro-cessing program may have a special tool for formatting envelopes.

Mr. Thomas Marks
112 Estes Street
San Antonio, TX 00000

The addressee's name should appear in the center of the envelope, so begin typ-ing five to ten spaces left of center, depending on the length of the name. The name, title, and address of the person receiving the letter should be the same as the inside address of the letter. The form should also be identical. Thus, if an attention line is used in the letter, then it should also be included on the enve-lope. The two-letter Postal Service abbreviations are used for the state. Several forms are acceptable:

Form	Sample
Name, Title	Mr. Gabriel Aaron, President
Organization	Kessler Records
Street	11 Noah Road
City, State ZIP	Dylan, MN 00000
Name	Mr. Gabriel Aaron
Title	President
Organization	Kessler Records
Department	Sales Division
Street	11 Noah Road
City, State ZIP	Dylan, MN 00000
Organization	Kessler Records
Department	Sales Division
Attention line	Attention: Gabriel Aaron
Street	11 Noah Road
City, State ZIP	Dylan, MN 00000
Name	Mr. Gabriel Aaron
In care of	In care of Frank Courtney
Street	11 Noah Road
City, State ZIP	Dylan, MN 00000

In cases of dual addresses, where a company may have both a street address and a box number, the Postal Service will deliver the letter to the lower address:

Name	Mr. Gabriel Aaron
Organization	Kessler Records
Building/Street	11 Noah Road
Box	Post Office Box 54
City, State ZIP	Dylan, MN 00000

Foreign Addresses

Styles vary in foreign countries. If possible, type a foreign address in the same form as the return address of the correspondence from abroad. The name of the country should appear in capitals.

Special Instructions

If mailing or special instructions appear in the letter, then they should also be typed on the envelope. Special messages for the reader—CONFIDENTIAL, IMMEDIATE ACTION, or PERSONAL—should be typed ten lines below the top in the left-hand corner. Special mailing instructions—SPECIAL DELIV-ERY, CERTIFIED, or REGISTERED—should be typed in capitals below the stamps.

Dr. Derek Hinton
33 Bailey Road
Pierre, SD 00000

CONFIDENTIAL   CERTIFIED MAIL

Mr. Michael Joseph, President
Weiner Marketing
14 Madeleine Boulevard
San Antonio, TX 00000

Envelope Size

Business envelopes come in two popular sizes:

No. $6\frac{3}{4}$ $3\frac{5}{8}'' \times 6\frac{1}{2}''$
No. 10 $4\frac{1}{8}'' \times 9\frac{1}{2}''$

Window Envelopes

When you use window envelopes, make sure that you center the address within the window so that the margin on each side is at least one quarter of an inch.

Postal Service Requirements

For machine processing, the U.S. Postal Service recommends typing the envelope address in capitals without punctuation:

MR GABRIEL AARON
KESSLER RECORDS
11 NOAH ROAD
DYLAN MN 00000

For optical scanning equipment, the Postal Service has set certain limits to the size of the envelope:

Height: $6\frac{1}{8}$"

Length: $11\frac{1}{2}$"

Thickness: $\frac{1}{4}$"

Both $6\frac{3}{4}$ and No. 10 envelopes fit these requirements.

For optical character recognition, the address should fit within a box $2\frac{3}{8}$" $\times$ 7". The margins should be at least 1" on the sides and $\frac{5}{8}$" on the bottom. For bar coding, the lower-right-hand corner should leave a $\frac{5}{8}$" $\times$ $4\frac{1}{4}$" margin.

Chapter 11

Forms of Address

The following are conventional forms of address in general use. You can use them as a guide for correspondence, specifically for envelopes and salutations.

Note that all presidential and federal and state elective officials are addressed as *Honorable*. A person once entitled to *Governor*, *Judge*, *General*, *Honorable* or a similar distinctive title may retain the title for his or her lifetime.

Academic titles or professional titles replace *Mr.* or *Ms.* Don't use two titles with the same meaning with one name: *Dr. Paula White* or *Paula White, M.D.*, not *Dr. Paula White, M.D.* or *Ms. Paula White, M.D.* Spell out all titles in an address except *Dr.*, *Mr.*, *Mrs.* and *Ms.* Use *Ms.* for women generally, unless the woman addressed has expressed a preference for *Miss* or *Mrs.*

Addressee	*Envelope*	*Salutation*
Ambassador, American	Honorable (surname) American Ambassador Address City, State	Sir: Madam: Dear Mr. Ambassador: Dear Madam Ambassador:
Ambassador, foreign	His (Her) Excellency (surname) Ambassador of Country Address Washington, D.C.	Excellency: Dear Mr. Ambassador: Dear Madam Ambassador: My dear Mr. (surname): My dear Madame (surname):

Addressee	*Envelope*	*Salutation*
Archbishop, Roman Catholic	The Most Reverend (surname) Archbishop of City Address City, State	Most Reverend and dear Sir: Dear Archbishop (surname): Dear Archbishop (surname): Your Excellency: Reverend Sir:
Bishop, Episcopal	The Right Reverend (surname) Bishop of Diocese Address City, State	Right Reverend Sir: Dear Bishop (surname):
Bishop, Methodist	Bishop (surname) Address City, State	My dear Bishop (surname): Dear Bishop (surname):
Bishop, Roman Catholic	The Most Reverend (surname) Bishop of Diocese Address City, State	Your Excellency: Most Reverend Sir: Dear Bishop (surname):
Cabinet Officer,	The Honorable (surname) The Secretary of (dept.) Address City, State	Sir: Madam: Dear Mr. Secretary: Dear Madam Secretary: Dear Mr. (surname): Dear Mrs. (surname):
Cardinal, Roman Catholic	His Eminence (given name) Cardinal (surname) Archbishop of (city) Address City, State	Your Eminence: My dear Cardinal: Dear Cardinal (surname):

Addressee	*Envelope*	*Salutation*
Clergyman, Protestant (except Episcopal)	The Reverend (Dr.) Name Address City, State	My dear Mr. (Dr.) (surname): Dear Mr. (surname): Dear Pastor (surname):
Consul	Full Name, Esq. Country Consul Address City, State	Sir: Madam: Dear Mr(s). Consul:
Dean, College	Dean (or Dr.) Name College or University Address City, State	Sir: Madam: Dear Dean (surname): Dear Dr. (surname):
Doctor	Dr. (surname) *or* Full Name, M.D., Ph.D., or D.D. Address City, State	Dear Dr. (surname):
Governor	The Honorable (surname) Governor of (state) Address City, State	Sir: Madam: My dear Governor (surname): Dear Governor (surname):
Imam	Imam Address City, State	Dear Imam (surname): Dear Imam:
Judge	The Honorable (surname) Name of Court Address City, State	Sir: Madam: My dear Judge (surname): Dear Judge (surname):

Addressee	*Envelope*	*Salutation*
Legislator	The Honorable (surname) Name of Legislative Body Address City, State	Sir: Madam: Dear Senator (surname): My dear Mr(s).: Dear Mr(s).: Dear Ms.:
Mayor	The Honorable (surname) Mayor of City Address City, State	Sir: Madam: Dear Mayor (surname):
Military Officer	Rank (surname) Address City, State	Sir: Madam: Dear (rank and surname):
President, College or University	President (full name) *or* Dr. (full name) College or University Address City, State	Sir: Madam: Dear Dr. (surname): Dear President (surname):
President, United States	The President The White House Washington, D.C.	Mr(s). President: Dear Mr(s). President: Dear President (surname):
President, Prime Minister (foreign country)	President (surname) *or* Prime Minister (surname) Address City, Country	Excellency: Dear Mr(s). President: Dear Mr. Prime Minister: Madame Prime Minister:
Priest, Roman Catholic, Episcopal	The Reverend (Dr.) (surname) Name of Church Address City, State	Reverend and dear sir: My dear Father (surname): Dear Father:

Addressee	*Envelope*	*Salutation*
Professor	Prof. (surname) Department of (subject) College or University Address City, State	Dear Sir: Dear Madam: Dear Professor (surname): Dear Dr. (surname):
Rabbi	Rabbi (surname) Name of synagogue Address City, State	Dear Rabbi (surname): Dear Dr. (surname):
Representative	The Honorable (surname) The House of Representatives Washington, D.C.	Sir: Madam: Dear Mr(s).(surname): Dear Mrs.(surname):
Senator	The Honorable (surname) United States Senate Washington, D.C.	Sir: Madam: Dear Senator (surname):
Supreme Court Justice	The Honorable (surname) Associate (or Chief) Justice of the United States Senate	Sir: Madam: Mr(s). Justice: Dear Mr(s). Justice: Dear Mr(s). Justice (surname):
United Nations	His (or Her) Excellency Country Representative to the United Nations United Nations New York, NY	Excellency: Your Excellency: Ambassador: Sir: Madam: Mr(s). (surname):

Addressee	*Envelope*	*Salutation*
Vice President	The Vice President Washington, D.C.	Sir: Madam: Dear Mr(s). Vice President: Dear Mr(s) (surname):

Chapter 12

Postal Service Abbreviations

As a general rule, spell out the names of U.S. states and territories when they are used alone or follow another name, such as that of a city, in ordinary text. If space is limited, if you are addressing an envelope, or if you are doing tabular work, use the official Postal Service abbreviations given below.

United States

Alabama	AL	Louisiana	LA	Ohio	OH
Alaska	AK	Maine	ME	Oklahoma	OK
Arizona	AZ	Maryland	MD	Oregon	OR
Arkansas	AR	Massachusetts	MA	Pennsylvania	PA
California	CA	Michigan	MI	Rhode Island	RI
Colorado	CO	Minnesota	MN	South Carolina	SC
Connecticut	CT	Mississippi	MS	South Dakota	SD
Delaware	DE	Missouri	MO	Tennessee	TN
District of		Montana	MT	Texas	TX
Columbia	DC	Nebraska	NE	Utah	UT
Florida	FL	Nevada	NV	Vermont	VT
Georgia	GA	New Hampshire	NH	Virginia	VA
Hawaii	HI	New Jersey	NJ	Washington	WA
Idaho	ID	New Mexico	NM	West Virginia	WV

United States (continued)

Illinois	IL	New York	NY	Wisconsin	WI
Indiana	IN	North Carolina	NC	Wyoming	WY
Iowa	IA	North Dakota	ND		
Kansas	KS				
Kentucky	KY				

United States Territories and Dependencies

Canal Zone	CZ	Puerto Rico	PR
Guam	GU	Virgin Islands	VI

Canadian Provinces

Alberta	AB	Nova Scotia	NS
British Columbia	BC	Ontario	ON
Labrador	LB	Prince Edward Island	PE
Manitoba	MB	Quebec	PQ
New Brunswick	NB	Saskatchewan	SK
Newfoundland	NF	Yukon Territory	YT
Northwest Territories	NT		

Chapter 13

Grammar Guide

Here is a concise review of the basic rules of English grammar. Use this guide as a quick reference for your business correspondence.

Parts of Speech

A word's use in the sentence determines its part of speech. For example, *light* may be a noun, verb, adjective, or adverb, depending how it is used.

Noun: Turn off the *light*.

Verb: Do not *light* the fire until sunset.

Adjective: The package is *light*.

Adverb: His favorite color is *light* blue.

Noun

A noun is a word that names a person, place, thing, or idea.

Person: George, Lincoln, Frank, Josie

Place: park, New York, London, garage

Thing: desk, apple, pen, table

Idea: truth, beauty, happiness, evil

Pronoun

A pronoun is a word that replaces a noun.

I, we, you, he, she, it, they, who, himself, herself, him, her, them

Verb

A verb is a word or group of words that expresses action or a state of being.

Action: run, write, sit, sleep, eat

State of being: am, is, are, was, were, will be

The verb, along with words that modify it or complete its meaning, forms the predicate, or verb phrase, of the sentence.

Adjective

An adjective describes or modifies a noun or pronoun.

lower floor, *higher* income, *green* truck, *simple* answer, *blue* sky

Adverb

An adverb modifies a verb, an adjective, or another adverb. It answers the questions where, how, when, or how much.

write *clearly, too* heavy, *very* high deficit, do it *later,* stay *here*

Preposition

A preposition relates a noun or pronoun to some other word in the sentence.

at, in, to, from, of, near, by, toward, with

Conjunction

A conjunction joins words, phrases, or clauses.

and, but, or, nor since, although

Interjection

An interjection expresses strong feeling.

Oh! No! Shhh!

Phrases and Clauses

Phrases and clauses are groups of words that function as a unit of grammar; they may function as a noun, verb, adjective, or adverb.

Clause

A clause is a group of words that contains a subject and a verb. A clause may be either *independent* or *dependent*.

An independent, or main, clause makes a complete statement. It can stand alone as a simple sentence.

> I am.

> The secretary sent the report last week.

A dependent clause cannot stand alone as a sentence, but is subordinate to the independent clause. Dependent clauses are of several types:

> Adjective: This is the agent *who handles shipping*.

> Adverb: *When you finish typing the letter,* you should mail it immediately.

> Noun: *Whoever needs security passes* should send a request to the office.

> Relative (pronoun): The reporter *who filed the story* did not leave his name.

Phrase

A phrase is a group of related words that functions as a grammatical unit but does not include a subject and verb. A phrase may work as a part of speech.

> Verb phrase: Frank *has been working late*.

> Prepositional phrase: Joe put the letters *in the mail*.

> Verbal phrase: We should start *selling lawn supplies*.

There are several types of verbal phrases, depending on the verb form that is used:

Participal: *Addressing the board,* he asked for patience.

Infinitive: She needed *to send the package today.*

Gerund: *Working overtime* will add to my income.

Types of Sentences

Simple Sentence

A simple sentence contains only one independent clause. A simple sentence may be short or very long if it has many phrases, a compound subject or verb, and a number of modifiers.

We won.

We won the contract for construction of the new office tower and will hire new staff to supervise the project.

Compound Sentence

A compound sentence has two or more independent clauses. Each of the clauses could stand alone as a simple sentence. They are joined by *and*, *or*, *but* or a semicolon (;). A compound sentence cannot contain a dependent clause.

We won, and they lost.

The company needs to expand into new markets, or it will have to close some divisions.

The president wants to expand into new markets; the chairman of the board recommended closing some divisions.

Complex Sentence

A complex sentence contains one independent clause and one or more dependent clauses.

When the company was faced with more losses, the president recommended expanding into new markets.

Compound-Complex Sentence

A compound-complex sentence contains at least two independent clauses and one or more dependent clauses.

> When profits fell for three quarters, the president recommended expansion into new markets, and the board of directors agreed.

Parts of the Sentence

The basic parts of the sentence are *subject, verb,* and *complement.* The sentence may include *modifiers*, which make the meaning more exact, and *connectives,* which create relationships between the parts.

Subject

The subject of a sentence is the word or group of words that names the thing, person, place, or idea about which the verb makes a statement. Most often, the subject is a noun or a pronoun.

> The *Director* called the meeting at noon. (noun)

> *She* asked the staff to attend. (personal pronoun)

Two verb forms—the gerund and, less often, the infinitive—can be the subject of a sentence.

> *Parking* is always a problem downtown. (gerund)

> *To park* a car requires less time than to take a bus. (infinitive)

> The demonstrative, interrogative, and indefinite pronouns can also be subjects.

> *That* will not solve the problem. (demonstrative)

> *What* are your plans for the future? (interrogative)

> *Everyone* is required to submit a form. (indefinite)

A phrase serving as a noun can function as a subject.

> *Replying to the proposal* will require a staff meeting.

> *To improve our marketing* remains a corporate goal.

An entire dependent clause can be used as a subject.

Whoever makes the highest sales will earn a bonus.

Whether the report has been released or not will determine our action.

Verb

A verb expresses an action or a state of being.

Action: John *runs*.

State of being: John *is* a runner.

Every sentence must contain a verb. A verb tells what the subject does, what happens to the subject, or what the subject is.

The manager *works* very hard.

The manager *has been overworked*.

The manager *is* a hard worker.

Number tells whether the verb is singular, referring to only one, or plural, referring to many. *Person* tells whether the first person, second person, or third person is performing the action. A verb and its subject must agree in number and person. Agreement is an essential principle of grammar in writing clear sentences.

	Singular	Plural
First	I	we
Second	you	you
Third	he, she, it	they

Tense indicates the time of an action—whether it happened in the past, the present, or the future.

Past: The office *was renovated* last year.

Present: The office *needs* renovation now.

Future: The office *will be renovated* next month.

Mood (indicative, imperative, subjunctive) denotes the manner of an assertion—whether it is a statement, command, wish, or condition.

Indicative: The company sells rubber widgets.

Imperative: Sell rubber widgets!

Subjunctive: If you could sell widgets, you would increase your profits.

Voice indicates whether the subject is performing or receiving the action of the verb. A verb in the *active voice* tells what the subject is doing; a verb in the *passive voice* tells what is being done to the subject.

Active voice: The technician operates all sound equipment.

Passive voice: The technician was fired for failing to report on time.

There are three types of verbs. The transitive verb takes a direct object, which is the object that receives the action of the verb. The intransitive verb takes does not take a direct object. The linking or copulative verb takes a predicate noun or a predicate adjective, which is a thing or quality that the verb connects to the subject.

Transitive: The player hits the ball.

Intransitive: The player fell down.

Linking: The player is a strong hitter.

Complement

The complement is a word or group of words that comes after the verb and completes its meaning. A complement may be a direct object of the verb, an indirect object of the verb, a predicative noun, or a predicative adjective.

(1) Direct object:

He gave the *directions* to his assistant.
Give *whatever directions that you have* to the assistant.

(2) Indirect object:

> He gave *her* the report.
> The truck driver did the *dispatcher* a big favor.

(3) Predicative noun:

The predicate noun, also called the predicate nominative or predicate complement, follows linking verbs and renames the subject. It can be a noun, a pronoun, a verb form, a phrase, or a clause.

Noun:	McDonald is chairman of the committee.
Pronoun:	The new employee is she.
Infinitive phrase:	The purpose of this memorandum is to clarify the report.
Noun clause:	The conference leader should be whoever is best qualified.

(4) Predicate adjective:

A predicate adjective occurs after linking verbs. It may be an adjective or an adjective phrase that modifies the subject.

> The flower smells sweet.

> The meeting on Tuesday will be short.

> He appears enthusiastic.

Modifiers

Modifiers—single words, phrases, or clauses—are used to limit, describe, or define some element of the sentence. They must attach as closely as possible to the word or phrase to which it refers. A modifier is said to dangle when it cannot attach both logically and grammatically to a definite word or phrase in the sentence.

Adjectives describe or limit the meaning of nouns or pronouns. A phrase may perform the function of an adjective.

> The *new* employee was given the *difficult* task of analyzing the *statistical* reports on the *income* tax. (adjectives)

The report *of the audit committee* is being studied. (prepositional phrase)

The report *submitted by the audit committee* is being studied. (verb phrase)

Adverbs modify verbs, adjectives, or other adverbs. They answer the questions where, how, how much, and when.

We will hold the meeting *here*. (where?)

She types *accurately*. (how?)

Spending *excessively*, he went bankrupt. (how much?)

Send the letter *now*. (when?)

Connectives

Connectives join one part of a sentence with another and show the relationship between the parts they connect. Conjunctions and prepositions are the most common connectives.

(1) Coordinators
Coordinate conjunctions—*and, but, or, nor, for, yet*—are perhaps the most frequently used connectives. They join sentences of equal grammatical importance—words with words, phrases with phrases, and independent clauses with independent clauses.

Wiener Computer sells hardware *and* software.

Management prefers to sell the division, *but* it will consider a restructuring.

The sales staff recommends renovating the store *or* moving to a new location.

Correlative conjunctions—*either...or, neither...nor, not only...but...also, both...and*—work in pairs to connect elements of a sentence. Each element of the sentence so connected should be a similar part of speech or construction. Thus, connect adjectives with adjectives, or noun phrases with noun phrases.

Either the manufacturer *or* the distributor bears responsibility.

Neither increasing inventory *nor* raising prices is an option.

Not only did the president attend, *but also* the chairman of the board came.

Conjunctive adverbs connect independent clauses and show the relationship between them. A logical relationship is established between the two clauses. Some conjunctive adverbs are *therefore, however, consequently, accordingly, furthermore, moreover,* and *nevertheless.*

Sales fell; *therefore* profits will decline. (cause and effect)

We will replace the part, however, we cannot pay the cost of labor. (contrast)

We hired new staff; *furthermore,* we added more office space. (addition)

(1) Subordinators

Subordinate conjunctions join dependent clauses to independent clauses. Some examples include *before, since, after, as, because, if, unless, until,* and *although.*

Before the snow storm hit us, sales of rock salt were low.

Because the recession is ending, the company is increasing production.

No department can hire new employees *until* new management arrives.

Construction will begin *after* the site inspection is completed.

Relative pronouns introduce noun and adjective clauses and also act as pronouns within the clause. These pronouns include *that, which, who, whom, whatever, whichever,* and *whoever.*

The officer *who patrols the parking lot* has filed a report.

Please note the date *that you will be leaving for vacation.*

Give the time cards to *whoever works part time.*

Relative adverbs introduce subordinate clauses. The most common of these connectives are *how, where, when,* and *while.*

He explained *how the company went bankrupt.*

When the stock rose, inside traders sold.

(2) Prepositions

A preposition shows the relationship between one word and another word, which is called the object of the preposition. The words following the preposition are called a prepositional phrase. Some common prepositions are *to, of, by, from, between, in, over, under,* and *for.*

The plane has arrived *from Hong Kong.*

For little more cost we can add color *to the brochure.*

Any expense *under fifty dollars* does not approval *from the supervisor.*

Try to avoid unnecessary prepositions.

Not: We will divide *up* the work.
But: We will divide the work.

Not: The water cooler was put near *to* the door.
But: The water cooler was put near the door.

Verbals

Verbals are words formed from verbs, but they do not function as verbs. The three verbal forms are the infinitive, participle, and gerund.

An infinitive, which is formed by adding *to* in front of the verb root, may function as a noun, adjective, or an adverb.

I need *to eat.*

To enroll requires a fifteen-dollar deposit.

The secretary needs *to type* the letters today.

A participle may be either a present participle, which is the *–ing* form, or a past participle, which is the *–ed* form. A participle acts as an adjective.

The *renting* party assumes responsibility for liability.

This season's *swimming* suits have been shipped.

The *burnt* building can be bought very cheaply.

A *broken* driveshaft was the problem.

A gerund is an *–ing* verb form that functions only as a noun.

Selling cheaply will generate more sales.

He knows that *exercising* will improve his health.

Nouns and Pronouns

A noun names a person, thing, place, or idea. They are most often the subjects of clauses or the objects of verbs or prepositions. Often an article (*the, a, an*) will precede them.

A proper noun names a particular place, person, or thing. Proper nouns should be capitalized.

Memphis, Mrs. Stella Johnston, Washington Monument, Gettysburg Address

A common noun names a member of a class or group of persons, places, or things. There is no need to capitalize a common noun.

apple, hope, seed, education, paper, asphalt

A collective noun is singular in form, but it names a group or collection of individuals. A collective noun may be used in a singular or plural sense. Whether used in a singular or plural sense, be consistent in subsequent use. Examples of collective nouns include *committee, jury, council, team,* and *task force.*

The jury files out. (one by one)

The jury fill out. (as a group)

Nouns may be concrete, referring to a particular or specific item, or abstract, referring to a class, quality, or state.

Specific: apple, secretary, notebook

Abstract: fruit, employee, thing, honesty, truth

Good writing tries to be as specific as possible.

Specific: The secretary must type the sales report.

Abstract: An employee must do the work.

Pronouns take the place of nouns. The personal pronoun shows which person (first, second, third) is the subject. Their form changes depending on the number, person, and case.

	Singular	Plural
First	I, me, my	we, us our
Second	you, you, your	you, you, your
Third	he, she, it; him, her, it; his, her, its	they, them, their

The relative pronoun takes the place of a noun in the clause it introduces and connects the clause with the rest of the sentence. Relative pronouns include *who, whom, which, that, what, whoever, whomever, whichever,* and *whatever.*

The interrogative pronoun has the same form as the relative pronoun, but its function differs. It asks a question. *Who* and *whom* refer to persons. *What* refers to things, and *which* refers to persons or things.

Which and *what* may also act as adjectives.

Which part needs replacement?

The meeting begins at *what* time?

The indefinite pronouns are singular forms that do not define a specific person or thing: *another, anyone, each, either, everyone, no one, nothing.*

The demonstrative pronouns point out or refer to a specific thing or something that is clearly implied. They include *this, that, these,* and *those.* They may be used as adjectives:

These items need to be returned to stock.

Or as pronouns:

> *This* cannot continue.

The reflexive pronouns are personal pronouns that emphasize or intensify a meaning. They are *myself, ourselves, yourself, yourselves, himself, herself, itself, themselves.*

> I *myself* authorized the promotion.

> The president *herself* made the request.

> Jack gave the package to the agent *himself.*

A reflexive pronoun is often the direct object of a verb. Its antecedent is the subject of the verb.

> I learned *myself* how to program computers.

> They hurt *themselves* when they overloaded the boat.

It may also be an indirect object.

> I bought *myself* a new laptop.

It may serve as object of a preposition.

> She finished the project by *herself.*

> He was beside *himself* with joy.

Do not use the reflexive pronoun in place of a shorter personal pronoun:

> Incorrect: Both the director and *myself* endorse the policy.
> Correct: Both the director and *I* endorse the policy.

Avoid the following pronoun errors:

> The use of *hisself* for *himself.*

> The use of *theirselves* for *themselves.*

Case

Case is the property of a noun or pronoun, which shows the relation of the word to other parts of the sentence. The word's position or a change in its form (inflection) indicates case. English has three cases: nominative, objective, and possessive.

All nouns and a few pronouns keep the same form in the nominative and objective cases. The position of the word in the sentence indicates its function. The change occurs only in the possessive:

The *ball* was hit by him. (nominative)

He hit *the ball*. (objective)

He is the *ball's* hitter. (possessive)

Pronouns, on the other hand, often are inflected (change form) as the case changes. Pronouns are very frequently misused because of problems with case.

We need a new computer. (nominative)

The computer was bought for *us*. (objective)

Our computer is new. (possessive)

Nominative Case

The nominative case is used primarily to name the subject of a verb or the complement that comes after a linking verb.

Either *she* or *I* will host the convention.

Harry, Mary, and *I* are attending.

Problems sometimes arise when pronouns are used in a grammatical construction called an appositive, a word or group of words that follow immediately and repeat the meaning of a word or phrase. The appositive should be in the same case as its antecedent.

The architects, *John and I*, have completed the plans.

The plans were passed to the architects, *John and me*.

Subject of a Verb in a Main Clause

A noun or pronoun serving as the subject of a verb is in the nominative case.

I am in charge.

When *he* missed the meeting, *she* took his place.

Neither *he* nor *I* knew the answer.

The reporters, *she* and *I,* wrote the article.

Subject of a Relative Clause

A relative pronoun (*who, whoever, which, whichever*) that is the subject of a clause is in the nominative case.

> Give the prize to *whoever writes the best essay.*

The clause itself may be a subject or an object. The case of the relative pronoun depends upon how it is used within the clause.

> The bonus will go to the person *who has the greatest sales increase.*

> *Whichever site is selected* will work well for us.

When the pronoun *who* is the subject of a verb, it is not affected by a parenthetical expression such as *I think, he believes,* or *they say* that may come between the subject and the verb.

> He is the person *who* I think is best qualified.

> We asked LaTanya, *who* we knew was familiar with the issue.

> Mr. Huang is the lawyer *who* we suppose will represent us in court.

Subject of Clause Introduced by Than or As

If the word following *than* or *as* introduces a clause, even if part of the clause is understood, that word must be in the nominative case. But if the word following *than* or *as* does not introduce a clause, it must be in the objective clause. To test whether the word should be in the nominative or objective case, complete the clause.

> He has been here longer than *she*. (has been here)

> Franco is a better typist than I. (am)

They were as late as *we* in filing the report. (were)

We were told as promptly as they. (were told)

In some cases, the word *than* or *as* may be in either the nominative or objective case, depending on what you intend to mean. To decide which case to use, complete the clause.

She likes the boss better than *I*. (like this boss)

She likes the boss better than *me*. (better than she likes me)

I have known Tyler as long as she. (has known Tyler)

I have known Tyler as long as her. (as I have known her)

Words Following Forms of Be

A noun or pronoun following a form of the verb *be* is in the nominative case. The word is called a predicate nominative or predicate noun. The word after a form of the verb *be* should be in the same case as the word before the verb. The verb form of *be* performs much as an equal (=) sign in mathematics.

They thought that I was *he*.

Is that *she?*

It was not *I* who took the phone call.

Be especially cautious in cases where there is a compound subject or predicate nominative. To test the proper pronouns, try reversing the sentence.

The new chairpersons are *he* and *I*.

He and *I* are the new chairpersons.

If any person wins the prize, it should be *he*.

If any person wins the prize, *he* should be it.

The winner was thought to be *I*.

I was thought to be the winner.

Objective Case

The objective case is used to name the object of the action of a verb, or the object of a preposition.

Object of the verb: The car struck *her.*

Object of the preposition: The letter was opened by *him.*

In cases where the object consists of a compound (more than one), make sure that all are in the objective case.

The chairman was seated between the president and *me.*

When you receive the check, please call either *him* or *her.*

The company promoted Bill and *me.*

If an appositive is used, it, too, should be in the objective case if its reference (antecedent) is in the objective case.

The director has appointed us, *you* and *me*, to the panel.

He gave *us* auditors the assignment.

Freedom is taken for granted by *us* Americans.

Direct Object of a Verb

A noun or pronoun serving as the direct object of a verb is in the objective case.

The limousine drove *him* to the airport.

My supervisor called *him* and *me* to the office.

They invited *us* to the reception.

I enjoyed meeting *them.*

The bank sent *us* acknowledgement of the deposit.

Indirect Object of a Verb

An action verb may have an indirect object, the destination of the direct object. The indirect object is also in the objective case.

The supervisor gave *me* the report.

The manager assigned *him* and *me* the task of writing the study.

A letter giving *him* the authority to represent us is being drafted.

Object of a Preposition

A noun or pronoun serving as the object of preposition is in the objective case.

He gave the report to *him*.

From *whom* did he receive the check?

The assignment was taken from *me* and given to *her*.

Be especially careful if the pronoun *between* takes a compound object. Do not say *between you and I*; say *between you and me*.

Just between *you* and *me*, I doubt that we will get that new account.

Possessive Case: Possessive with a Singular

The possessive case defines ownership. To form the possessive of singular words not ending in *s*, add an apostrophe followed by an *s*.

agent*'s* report; director*'s* office; secretary*'s* desk; anyone*'s* guess; somebody*'s* coat

If a singular word ends with an *s*, you may or may not add a final *s*. If the singular word seems to require an extra syllable to pronounce it, add the *s*.

boss*'s* office

waitress*'s* tip

two weeks*'* wages

4 hours*'* work

When a proper name ends with an *s*, follow the same guideline.

Charles*'* desk or Charles*'s* desk

James*'* letter or James*'s* letter

Delores' job or Delores's job

Roberts' house not Roberts's house

Possessive with a Plural

If the possessive is a plural that ends with s, add the apostrophe only.

district governors' meeting

supervisors' reports

schools' parking lots

Make sure that the apostrophe is placed properly in words where the plural form ends with an s.

ladies' room, not ladie's room

If the plural does not end with an s, simply add the 's as if it were singular

children's toys

women's fashions

Possessives and Contractions

Do not use apostrophes with possessive pronouns. *Its, whose,* and *theirs* are possessives that do not require an apostrophe. Do not confuse them with the contractions *it's, who's,* and *there's.* If unsure, read the sentence as *it is* or *who is* and see if it makes any sense.

I*ts* profit declined.

It's *hers.*

Whose profit declined?

Who's going?

Theirs are the best.

There's no reason to go.

Possessives with Compound Words

If combined words or phrases are possessives, punctuate them as if they were singular words. The apostrophe goes after the last word.

chief of staff*'s* recommendation

mother in law*'s* feelings

Jones and Smith*'s* offices

Follow the same rule if the compound word is plural.

notaries public*'s* seals

comptrollers general*'s* convention

When two or more people possess the same thing jointly, only the last word takes the possessive.

Bill and Sally*'s* car

Mary and John*'s* vacation

If one of the words in the joint possession is a pronoun, then all the words must be possessive.

Bill's and *her* new car

Mary's and *his* vacation

When two or more people possess something individually, then the possessive is formed on each word.

Bill*'s* and Sally*'s* cars

Jack*'s* and Ricardo*'s* assignment

When alternative possession is intended, each word must be in the possessive.

I wouldn't want either Ahmed*'s* or Reginald*'s* job.

Is that the author*'s* or the *editor's* opinion?

Some formal names do not require an apostrophe although they sound possessive.

> First Citizens Bank
>
> Harpers Ferry
>
> Pikes Peak

If the possessives are repeated in a sentence, use prepositional phrases to indicate possession for the sake of clarity.

> Not: The *committee's treasurer's report* was read.

> But: The *report of the committee's treasurer* was read.

Possessive with a Gerund

A noun or pronoun immediately preceding a gerund is in the possessive case.

> *Your* being late delayed the meeting.

> *Mr. Jones'* being late delayed the meeting.

> You can count on *his* doing a good job.

> *Carmela's* apologizing cleared the air.

Agreement and Reference

Many grammatical errors occur from failing to make different parts of a sentence agree in number, person, or gender.

The verb must agree with the subject in number and in person. If the subject is singular, the verb form must also be singular; if the subject is in the third person—*he, she, it*—the verb must also be in the third person. For this reason, you must identify the subject of the sentence and determine its person and number.

The pronoun must agree with its antecedent (the word to which it refers, also known as the referent) in number, person, and gender.

When writing a paragraph, make sure that you maintain consistency of number and person.

Subject Problems

The first step in making the parts of a sentence agree is to identify the subject. This task is not always as simple as it may seem. Here are some situations that present special problems.

Collective Words

A collective names a group of people or things. Although usually singular in form, a collective may be treated as either singular or plural according to the sense of the sentence.

A collective is singular when members of the group act, or are considered, as a unit.

> The Survey Committee *is visiting* the sites this week.

> The evaluation team *has* filed its final report.

> The news *is* bad.

A collective is plural when the members act, or are considered, as individuals.

> The jury *are* unable to agree on a verdict.

> The evaluation team *have* their differences to resolve before they file the report.

Common collectives include:

> assembly, association, audience, board, cabinet, class, commission, committee, company, corporation, council, counsel, counsel, couple, crowd, department, family, firm, group, jury, majority, minority, number, pair, press, public, staff, team, United States

Company names also qualify as collectives and may be either singular or plural. Usually, those ending with a singular sound are considered singular; those with a plural sound are considered plural.

> Flowers, Inc., *mails* its brochures through the postal service.

> Jackson Brothers *have sent* their agent to the meeting.

A name ending in *Company* or *Corporation*, though usually considered singular, may—if the sense of the sentence requires—be used in the plural.

> The Cleo Foundation *is* not on the list of tax-exempt corporations.

> The Factoid Corporation *report* first, followed by their subsidiaries.

When certain short words—*all, any, more, most, none, some, who, which*—are used as the subject of the sentence, they may be singular or plural depending on the intended meaning. When a prepositional phrase follows the word, the number of the noun in the phrase controls the number of the verb. When no such phrase follows, the writer may imply whether it is singular or plural by the choice of the verb.

> Some of the work *has been done.*

> Some of the returns *have been filed.*

> Most of the correspondence *is* routine.

> Most of the letters *are* acceptable.

> *Which* is to be posted? (which one?)

> *Which* are to be posted? (which ones?)

Check to see if your company uses a style manual; some guides suggest, for example, that *none* is always singular while others regard it as always plural. *None* means *no one*, but if followed by a prepositional phrase with a plural object, it implies more than one. One possibility to avoid this problem is to substitute the phrase *not one of.*

> None of the items *is* deductible.

> None of the items *are* deductible.

> Not one of the items *is* deductible.

Units of Measure

When a number is used with a plural noun to indicate a unit of measurement—*money, time, fractions, portions, distance, weight, quantity,* and so on—a singular verb is used. When the term is thought of as individual parts, a plural verb is used.

Twenty dollars is due on April 3.

Twenty dollars are in the stack.

Ten years seems like a long time.

Ten years have gone by since I changed jobs.

Twenty-one is our quota for each day.

Twenty-one pages are needed to finish the report.

When fractions and expressions—*rest of, the remainder of, a part of, percent of,* and so on—are followed by a prepositional phrase, the noun or pronoun in that phrase governs the number of the verb.

Four-fifths of the job *was* finished on time.

Four-fifths of the letters *were* finished on time.

The *remainder* of the work *is* due on Friday.

The *remainder* of the reports *are* due on Friday.

What *percent* of the information *was* lost?

What *percent* of the items *were* lost?

Confusing Singular and Plural Forms

Whether a word is singular or plural may not be easy to determine. Some words that end in *s* may be singular, and some seemingly singular words may be plural.

These words are singular, though they are plural in form: apparatus, news, physics, summons, and whereabouts.

The *news* is disturbing.

His *whereabouts* has not yet been made known.

Physics is a difficult course.

Other words are plural although they are singular, or collective, in meaning:

assets, earnings, means (income), odds, premises, proceeds, quarters, savings, wages, winnings

His *assets* are listed on the statement.

Earnings are up this quarter.

The *odds* are against us.

The *proceeds* are earmarked for the fund.

These words may be either singular or plural, depending on their meaning, even though they are plural in form:

ethics, goods, gross, headquarters, mechanics, politics, series, species, statistics, tactics

Ethics is the subject of his lecture.

His business *ethics* are above question.

Statistics is the only course I failed in school.

The *statistics* prove that I am right.

A *series* of errors has marked our efforts.

A *series* of lucky breaks are our last hope.

Indefinite Pronouns

These indefinite pronouns are singular. When they are used as subjects, they require singular verbs. When they are antecedents, the pronouns should also be singular.

Anybody, anyone, any one, anything, each, either, every, everybody, everyone, every one, everything, neither, nobody, no one, nothing, one, somebody, some one, something

Anyone is welcome as long as *he* behaves.

Each of us *is* obliged to sign *his* name.

Either of the alternatives *is* suitable.

Everything seems to be working well.

Neither of the plans *is* acceptable.

Someone has to finish the project.

When *each* or *every* is used to modify a compound subject, the subject is considered singular.

> *Every* supervisor and manager *has* submitted a schedule.

> *Each* dog and cat is required to wear its own name tag.

These words are plural:

> Both, few, many, several, others

> *Both* of us *have received our* new assignments.

> *Few were* able to finish *their* work.

> *Several* of the divisions *have met their* quotas.

Pronoun Agreement with He or She

When the gender of a noun or pronoun antecedent is not known, the custom in English is to use the masculine personal pronoun *he*.

> Each child (boy or girl) develops at *his* own pace.

The trend is to be as inclusive of gender as possible so that neither men nor women feel excluded. You may wish to use a form of *he* and *she*.

> Each child develops at *his or her* own pace.

This usage is generally accepted, but it is wordy. One possibility is to change the sentence to the plural.

> All children develop at their own pace.

Some grammar authorities permit the use of the plural pronoun *their* even when the indefinite pronoun is plural.

> Each child develops at *their* own pace.

Others will commonly use the feminine.

> Each develops at *her* own pace.

Whatever choice is made, the most important point is to be consistent. Your company may prefer one style or another.

Relative Pronouns

The verb in a relative clause must agree in number and in person with the relative pronoun (*who, which, that, what*) that serves as the subject of the clause. The relative pronoun, in turn, must agree with its antecedent. Before you can make the verb agree with the relative pronoun, you must first find the antecedent and determine its person and number.

> Have you talked with the person *who was* waiting to see you? (*Person* is the antecedent of the relative pronoun *who,* and the verb *was* agrees with it, third person and singular.)

> Where are the books *that were* ordered? (*Books* is the antecedent of the relative pronoun *that,* and the verb *were* agrees with it, third person and plural.)

> We *who have* met him do not doubt his ability. (*We* is the antecedent of the relative pronoun *who,* and the verb *have* agrees with it, first person and plural.)

In sentences that contain the phrases *one of the* or *one of those,* the antecedent of the relative pronoun is not *one,* but the plural words that follow.

> One of the letters *that were* on my desk is missing.

> He is one of those managers *who are* moving up the corporate ladder.

> One of the delegates *who are* attending the meeting has a phone call.

Who, that, or *which* may refer to a collective noun. When the members of the group are considered as a unit, either *that* or *which* should be used—*that* is usually preferred if the group comprises persons rather than things. *Who* is used when the persons comprising a group act or are considered as individuals.

> He reports on behalf of a *group* of citizens *that* opposes the plan.

> We have heard from an *association* of homeowners *who* support re-zoning.

Subjects Joined by And

When two or more subjects are joined by *and,* whether the subjects are singular or plural, they form a compound subject, which is considered plural.

The *date and the time* of the meeting *have* not been set.

The *director and his administrators are* bringing *their* staffs.

He and I are making a personal appeal.

The *letters, reports, and other papers are* where you left *them.*

The same rule applies when two or more phrases or clauses serve as a compound subject.

Raising the rent and lowering costs will add to the profits.

That you increased sales and that you extended your hours are factors to consider.

There are some exceptions to the rule that a compound subject joined by *and* takes a plural verb. The compound may represent a single idea and is thus considered singular.

Ham and eggs is a typical American breakfast.

Growth and development has increased dramatically.

An article or personal pronoun helps determine whether the compound subject is singular or plural.

My teacher and friend guides me always. (one person)

My teacher and my friend guide me always. (two people)

Subjects Joined by Or or Nor

When singular subjects are joined by *or* or *nor*, the subject is considered singular.

Neither the *director nor the assistant director knows* that *he* is scheduled to attend the conference.

One or the other of us *has* to go.

When one singular and one plural subject are joined by *or* or *nor*, the subject closer to the verb determines the number of the verb.

Either the CD or the *floppy disks have* the file that you need.

Either the floppy disks or the CD *has* the file that you need.

When one antecedent is singular and the other antecedent is plural, the pronoun agrees with the closer antecedent.

Is it director or the *secretaries who merit* praise?

Is it the secretaries or the *director who merits* praise?

When the subjects joined by *or* or *nor* differ in person, the subject nearer the verb determines its person.

I was told that either she or *you were* to be responsible.

I was told that either you or *she was* to be responsible.

To clarify any potential misunderstanding, try to place the verb as closely as possible to its subject.

Shifts in Number or Person

Once you establish a word as either singular or plural, keep it the same throughout the sentence. Be sure that all verbs and all pronouns referring to that word agree with it in number.

Not: A *person needs* someone to turn to when *they are* in trouble.
But: A *person needs* someone to turn to when *he or she is* in trouble.

Not: When *one* has to work overtime, *they* deserve a bonus.
But: When *one* has to work overtime, *one* deserves a bonus.

Be consistent. If you decide that a collective noun is singular, keep it singular throughout the sentence. Make sure that all verbs and pronouns that refer to it are also singular. The same is true if the collective noun is plural.

The committee *has* announced *its* decision.

The committee *have* adjourned and gone to *their* offices.

Our staff is always glad to offer *its* advice and help.

Avoid shifting the person of the pronoun, which refers to the same antecedent.

Not: When *one* is happy, everyone around *you* seems happy, too.
But: When *one* is happy, everyone around *one* seems happy, too.

Not: As the *ship* entered *her* berth, *its* crew secured the lines.
But: As the *ship* entered *its* berth, *its* crew secured the lines.
Or: As the *ship* entered *her* berth, *her* crew *secured* the lines.

Structure Problems

Usually the person and number of a subject or antecedent are easy to identify. Occasionally a puzzling sentence appears. The structure of the sentence leads us to believe that the subject is a different word than it actually is.

Verb Precedes Subject

When the verb precedes the subject in the sentence, locate the subject and make the verb agree with it.

Are the *file cabinet and the bookcase* in the warehouse?

Walking down the hall *are* the *men* we are expecting.

Clearly visible on the desk *were* the *papers* missing from the file.

From these books *come some* of our best *ideas.*

Among those attending *were* two former *presidents* of the company.

To us *falls* the *task* of compiling the data.

When, here, and *there*, when introducing a sentence, do not influence the number or person of the verb. In such sentences, find the subject and make the verb agree with it.

Where *are* the breakout *sessions* to be held?

Where *is* the *case* filed?

Here *are* the *messages* for which we were waiting.

Here *is* the *message* for which we were waiting.

There *are* two *books* on the shelf.

There *is* a *book* on the shelf.

What, who, which, the interrogative pronouns, do not affect the number of the verb. Again, find the subject of the sentence and make the verb agree with it.

What *is* the *status* of the Florez case?

What *are* your *recommendations?*

Who in this group *are members* of your staff?

It as subject takes a singular verb.

It is solutions that we want, not more problems.

It is doubtful that he will arrive today.

There is not the subject, but the verb agrees with the subject that follows it.

There *are five copies* enclosed in the envelope.

There *is one copy* enclosed in the envelope.

Words Between Subject and Verb

The presence of explanatory or parenthetical phrases, or other modifiers, between the subject and verb does not change the number or person of the subject. Once again, find the real subject of the sentence and make sure that the verb agrees with it.

His sworn *statement*, together with copies of the testimony and statements from other parties connected with the case, *was* made part of the record.

The *amount* shown, plus interest, *is* due within thirty days.

The *letter* with its several attachments *was* received this morning.

Our *writings,* like our speech, *are* signs of our education.

The *supervisor,* instead of the agents who have been assigned to the case, *is* scheduled to visit.

No *one* but those present *knows* this information.

Subject and Predicate Differ in Number

After forms of the verb *to be,* you may often find a construction called the predicate nominative, a word or phrase that means the same as the subject. If the subject and predicate nominative differ in number, the verb agrees with the subject.

The problem *was* insufficient funds.

Insufficient funds *were* the problem.

One issue *is* the statistical surveys.

Statistical surveys *are* one issue.

Parallel Constructions

Similar ideas should be expressed in similar grammatical forms.

Not: *Singing* and *to dance* are not permitted.
But: *Singing* and *dancing* are not permitted.

Not: This term the students are learning the value of *courtesy* and *being kind.*
But: This term the students are learning the value of *courtesy* and *kindness.*

Not: His main virtues are *his generosity* and *that he is sincere.*
But: His main virtues are *generosity* and *sincerity.*
But: His main virtues are *that he is generous* and *that he is sincere.*

Special Problems of Pronoun Reference
Ambiguous Antecedents

Sometimes a reader may be confused by the antecedent of a pronoun. To whom does the pronoun refer? Do not use forms of the same pronoun to refer to different antecedents. Make sure that the reference is obvious.

Not: The director told Mr. Lopez that *he* would have to make *his* trip to Boston in June. (Who has to make the trip to Boston in June? The director or Mr. Lopez?)

But: The director has to make a trip to Boston in June, and he so informed Mr. Lopez.

Place the pronoun as close as possible to its antecedent to avoid ambiguity or confusion.

Not: The letter is on the conference table *that* we received yester-day.

But: The letter *that* we received yesterday is on the conference table.

Indefinite Antecedents

Be sure that the reference to an antecedent is quite specific.

Not: The copies of these letters were not initialed by the writers, so we are returning *them*. (What is being returned, the copies, the letters, or the writers?)

But: We are sending back the copies of the letters because *they* were not initialed.

Not: When you have finished the book and written your review, please bring *it* to the library.

But: When you have finished the book and written your review, please bring the book to the library.

Implied Antecedents

As a general rule, the antecedent of a pronoun must appear in the sentence and not merely be implied. And the antecedent should be a specific word, not an idea expressed in a phrase or a clause. *It, which, this,* and *that* are the pronouns that most often confuse. Too often the reader cannot find the reference that may be perfectly clear to the writer.

Not: Although the doctor operated at once, *it* was not a success and the patient died.

But: Although the doctor performed an *operation* at once, *it* was not a success and the patient died.

Not: This matter has also been examined by the accounting depart-ment, a copy of *which* is attached.

But: This matter has also been examined by the accountants. A copy of the report that we gave them is attached.

Vague Reference

Using impersonal pronouns—*it, they,* and *you*—may produce vague, wordy sentences.

Not: In the manual *it* says to make two copies.
But: The manual says to make two copies.

Not: *They* say we will have a cold, wet week ahead.
But: The weatherman predicts a cold, wet week ahead.

Not: From this report *you* can identify clearly the cause of the accident.
But: This report identifies clearly the cause of the accident.

Verbs

Tense refers to time. Verbs describe an action or a state of being, but verbs also tell *when* the action takes place or *when* the state exists. The time dimension of verbs is called *tense*. We indicate tense by changing the verb itself or by adding an auxiliary verb.

English has six tenses: three simple tenses (present, past, and future) and three perfect tenses, which indicate that an action is completed. The perfect tenses use a compound verb.

Present tense:	I walk, he walks
Present perfect tense:	I have walked, he has walked
Past tense:	I walked, he walked
Past perfect tense:	I had walked, he had walked
Future tense:	I shall walk, he will walk
Future perfect tense:	I shall have walked, he will have walked

Each of the six tenses also has a progressive form, which indicates an action is continuing. The progressive consists of a form of the verb *to be* and the present participle (the *–ing* form of the verb).

Present tense:	I am walking, he is walking
Present perfect tense:	I have been walking, he has been walking

Past tense:	I was walking, he was walking
Past perfect tense:	I had been walking, he had been walking
Future tense:	I shall be walking, he will be walking
Future perfect tense:	I shall have been walking, he will have been walking

The present tense and the past tense also have an emphatic form, which uses *do, does,* and *did* as auxiliaries.

| Present tense: | I do understand, she does understand |
| Past tense: | You did understand, they did understand |

Regular and Irregular Verbs

Verbs are classified as regular and irregular according to the way that they form their principal parts.

Present:	arrive, know
Past:	arrived, knew
Past participle:	arrived, known

Regular verbs form their past tense and past participle by adding *–ed* to the infinitive (root) of the verb:

Present	*Past*	*Past participle*
talk	talked	talked
help	helped	helped
jump	jumped	jumped

Irregular verbs change their form when forming the principal parts.

Present	*Past*	*Past participle*
see	saw	seen
say	said	said
write	wrote	written

Principal Parts of Troublesome Verbs

Note that some verbs may have more than one acceptable forms in the past or the past participle. The perfect tenses are formed by adding an auxiliary verb before the past participle: *has* or *have* for the present perfect, and *had* for the past perfect.

Present	*Past*	*Perfect*
arise	arose	have arisen
bear	bore	have borne
begin	began	have begun
bid	bade	have bid, bidden
bleed	bled	have bled
broadcast	broadcast(ed)	have broadcast(ed)
burst	burst	have burst
choose	chose	have chosen
cling	clung	have clung
dig	dug	have dug
drown	drowned	have drowned
drink	drank	have drunk
flee	fled	have fled
fling	flung	have flung
fly	flew	have flown
flow	flowed	have flowed
forsake	forsook	have forsaken
freeze	froze	have frozen
hang (a picture)	hung	have hung
hang (a person)	hanged	have hanged
lay (place)	laid	have laid
lead	led	have led
lend	lent	have lent
lie (rest)	lay	have lain
light	lit, lighted	have lit, lighted
raise	raised	have raised
rid	rid, ridded	have rid, ridded
ring	rang	have rung

set	set	have set
sew	sewed	have sewed, sewn
shrink	shrank, shrunk	have shrunk, shrunken
sink	sank, sunk	have sunk
sit	sat	have sat
ski	skied	have skied
slay	slew	have slain
sleep	slept	have slept
slide	slid	have slid, slidden
sling	slung	have slung
slink	slunk	have slunk
smite	smote	have smitten
spring	sprang, sprung	have sprung
steal	stole	have stolen
sting	stung	have stung
stink	stank, stunk	have stunk
stride	strode	have stridden
strive	strove	have striven
swim	swam	have swum
swing	swung	have swung
throw	threw	have thrown
thrust	thrust	have thrust
weave	wove	have woven
wring	wrung	have wrung
write	wrote	have written

Past Tense vs. Past Perfect Tense

The past perfect tense indicates that an action was completed (perfected) earlier than another action in the past. The past perfect tense thus differs from the simple past tense.

> When I *returned* from lunch, she *finished* the letter. (Both *returned* and *finished* occurred at the same time in the past.)

> When I *came* back from lunch, she *had finished* the letter. (Both actions were in the past, but *had finished* means the action was completed before the person *returned*.)

We *discovered* that the police car *was following* us. (Both *discovered* and *was following* occurred at the same time in the past.)

We *discovered* that the police car *had been following* us. (They *discovered* about the police car some time after it *had been following* them.)

Mood

The mood of a verb describes the kind of statement is being made. The mood may be indicative (factual statement); imperative (demand); or subjunctive (hypothetical or contrary to fact).

Indicative: She types the letter.

Imperative: Type the letter now!

Subjunctive: If she only would type the letter, we would not have to complain.

The Indicative Mood

The indicative mood makes a statement or asks a question. It is the most common mood in writing.

The conference *was scheduled* for Tuesday.

What *is* the correct answer?

From the evidence the attorney *feels* that the company has no case.

The Imperative Mood

The imperative mood expresses a command, a request, or a suggestion. The subject of an imperative sentence is most often the pronoun *you*, although it is usually implied and not expressed. Imperative statements may end with an exclamation point for emphasis.

Lock the safe before you leave the office.

Help the staff learn the safety procedures.

Please *sign* the forms as soon as possible.

Do not *accept* unauthorized shipments!

In business writing, an imperative indicates that an action is an order.

Please *forward* this report promptly.

Return all unsold merchandise to the distributor.

Reduce payrolls at once.

The Subjunctive Mood

The subjunctive expresses a wish, an indirect command, or a condition contrary to fact. The subjunctive is less commonly used now in English, but it can still be seen in certain situations.

Indicative: The manager *prepares* his report immediately.

Subjunctive: We suggested that the manager *prepare* his report immediately

Indicative: The plane usually *arrives* on time.

Subjunctive: *Should* the plane *arrive* on time, we will make the connection.

The subjunctive is used after forms of the verb *to be*.

The boss requested that we *be* there.

If I *were* president, I would spend more on education.

If he *were* capable of completing the job, I am sure he would.

The subjunctive is used to express a wish that is not likely to be fulfilled or impossible to realize.

The bank wishes it *were* possible to grant a loan at this time.

The committee wishes he *were* here to defend his position.

Would that I *were* able take your place.

The subjunctive is commonly employed to indicate a motion at a meeting.

I move that the meeting *be* adjourned.

Resolved, that a committee *be* appointed to study this issue.

In a subordinate clause after a verb that expresses a command, a request, or a suggestion, the subjunctive is appropriate.

The chairman asked *that* the memo *be* distributed in duplicate.

We suggest *that* the treasurer *be* relieved of responsibility for petty cash.

The customer asks *that* the company *consider* a full refund.

The subjunctive expresses a condition that is contrary to fact.

If I *were* in Paris, I would eat very well.

If this case *were* simple, we would have solved it long ago.

If I *were* you, I would take the job offer.

In formal writing and speech, the subjunctive is used after *as if* or *as though* expressions. The statement that follows is not factual.

The man talked *as if* he *were* an expert on taxation.

This report looks *as though* it *were* the work of a college freshman.

Voice

Voice indicates whether the subject of the verb is performing or receiving the action of the verb. The two voices are active and passive.

Active: He hit the ball.

Passive: The ball was hit by him.

If the subject is performing the action, the verb is in the active voice.

The director *approved* our time card.

The report *summarizes* the committee's recommendations.

The agent *asked* the taxpayers to bring their receipts.

If the subject is being acted upon, the verb is in the passive voice. The passive form always consists of a form of the verb *to be*.

Our schedule *was approved* by the director.

The committee's recommendations *were summarized* in the report.

The taxpayers *were asked* by the agent to bring their receipts.

In general, the active voice is preferred to the passive. The active voice is less wordy and more direct. The passive voice is often used in technical and scientific writing. Try to avoid employing it excessively.

Shifts in Voice

Shifts in voice—often accompanied by shifts in subject—usually occur in compound or complex sentences.

Not: As I *searched* through the files for the memorandum, the missing report *was found.*
But: As I *searched* through the files for the memorandum, I *found* the missing report.

Modifiers
Classification of Modifiers

Modifiers fall generally into two categories: adjectival and adverbial. These may consist of a single word or a phrase or clause.

Adjectives describe, limit, or make more exact the meaning of a noun or pronoun.

Adverbs describe, limit, or make more exact the meaning of a verb, an adjective, or another adverb.

Articles

Articles are a type of adjective. The definite articles are *a* and *an*, and the indefinite article is *the*. Use *a* before words beginning with a consonant sound, *an* before those beginning with a vowel sound.

a desk, *a* book

an agent, *an* error, *an* unusual occurrence

The article before two connected nouns or adjectives indicate whether the words refer to different things or people.

We elected *a* secretary and *a* treasurer. (two persons)

We elected *a* secretary and treasurer. (one person with two positions)

In stock we have *a* black and gray. (one unit with two colors)

In stock we have *a* black and *a* gray. (two units in two colors)

Do not use *a* or *an* after *sort of, kind of, manner of, style of,* or *type of.*

Not: What *kind of a* book do you want?
But: What *kind of book* do you want?

Do not use *the* before *both.*

Not: We'll buy *the* both of them.
But: We'll buy *both* of them.

Adverbs with Two Forms

Some adverbs have two forms—one ending in *–ly,* the other not. The longer form is nearly always acceptable and is preferable in formal writing. The short form is properly used in brief, forceful sentences (in commands, such as the road sign "Drive Slow") and may be used informally. The *–ly* form should, however, always be used to modify an adjective.

The following adverbs have two forms:

slow, slowly	clear, clearly	quick, quickly
cheap, cheaply	sharp, sharply	loud, loudly
soft, softly	deep, deeply	direct, directly

Sometimes the desired meaning will determine the form that should be used. For example, either *direct* or *directly* may be used when the meaning is "in a straight line," but *directly* is the only choice when *soon* is meant.

In informal speech sometimes the *–ly* is dropped from the adverb. This usage is not appropriate for writing.

We are *really* glad that you have accepted. (not *real* glad)

Comparison of Adjectives and Adverbs
Degrees of Comparison

Adjectives and adverbs change form to show differences in degree. That is, they have a positive form that changes if it is used to make a comparison or a superlative.

Positive Degree

The positive degree directly names the quality that the adjective or adverb expresses.

> *high* morale, a *dependable* worker, work *fast*, prepare *carefully*

Comparative Degree

The comparative degree indicates that a quality exists to a lesser or greater degree between two things. It is formed by adding *–er* to the positive degree or by inserting *more* or *less* before the positive form.

> The sales department has *higher* morale than the purchasing department.
>
> Juanita is a *more dependable* worker than Harold.
>
> Luis can work *faster* than Toni.
>
> This plan was prepared *more carefully* than the previous effort.

Superlative Degree

The superlative degree denotes the greatest or the least amount of the quality among three or more things. It is formed by adding *–est* to the positive degree of the adverb or adjective or by inserting *most* or *least* before the positive form.

> The sales department has the *highest* morale of any department.
>
> Juanita is the *most dependable* worker in the company.
>
> Luis can work *fastest* of all.
>
> This plan was the *most carefully* planned effort that I have ever seen.

Do not confuse the comparative degree and the superlative degree. Again, the comparative refers only to two things; the superlative, to more than two.

This book is the *longer* of the two.

This book is the *longest* of the three.

Using –er and –est or More and Most

The meanings of *–er* and *more* and *–est* and *most* do not differ. In some cases either may be used. However, most adjectives of three syllables or more and almost all adverbs use *more* and *most* (or *less* and *least*) rather than *–er* and *–est* in the comparisons. Adding *–er* or *–est* tends to stress the *quality* while adding *more* or *most* tends to emphasize the *degree* of the comparison.

Should I have been *kinder* or *harsher* in handling that call?

That report is the *longest* of the three.

Should I have been *more firm* or *less firm* in handling the caller?

Of all the forms, this one is the *most simple* and that one is the *least simple* to fill out.

Irregular Comparisons

In some cases the adverb or adjective may change form when used as a comparison or a superlative.

Positive	*Comparative*	*Superlative*
good	better	best
well	better	best
bad (ill, evil)	worse	worst
badly (ill)	worse	worst
far	farther	farthest
late	later	latest, last
little	less, lesser	least
many, much	more	most

Problems with Comparison
Adjectives and Adverbs That Cannot be Compared

Some adjectives and adverbs express qualities that are not subject to comparison. They represent the highest degree of a quality and, as a result, cannot be improved. Some of these words are listed below:

complete	infinitely	square
correct	perfect	squarely
dead	perfectly	supreme
deadly	perpendicularly	totally
exact	preferable	unique
horizontally	round	uniquely
immortally	secondly	universally

Unique is commonly used as a superlative. *Unique* means that it is the only one, and therefore one cannot say it is *most unique*.

Not: Her voice is the *most unique* that I have ever heard.
But: Her voice is *unique*.

Incomplete Comparison

When you make a comparison between two items, make sure that both terms of the comparison are named. Whenever a comparison is not completed, the meaning of the sentence is obscured.

Not: Juan's letter states the problem better than Maria.
But: Juan's letter states the problem better than Maria's.

Not: Juan's proposed form is less complicated than management.
But: Juan's proposed form is less complicated than that of management.

Not: I have known him longer than Juan.
But: I have known him longer than I have known Juan.

Not: I enjoy this kind of work more than Juan.
But: I enjoy this kind of work more than Juan does.

Split Infinitive

Inserting an adverb between *to* and the rest of an infinitive creates a split infinitive. Whenever possible, try to avoid splitting an infinitive.

Not: He wished to *completely* forget the matter.
But: He wished to forget the matter *completely*.

Dangling Phrases

A dangling phrase is one that does not refer to any part of the sentence. Revise the dangling phrase by connecting it to a noun or pronoun in the sentence or by rewriting the phrase. A dangling modifier is most often a form of the verb, either an infinitive (*to be*) or a participle (*-ing*).

Dangling: *To do well in this course,* careful *study* is necessary.
Improved: *To do well in this course,* you must study carefully.
Improved: *If you want to do well in this course, you* must study carefully.

Dangling: *Rushing to meet the deadline,* the report was poorly prepared.
Improved: *Rushing to meet the deadline,* they prepared the report poorly.

Dangling: *To apply for a position,* the form must be filled out.
Improved: *To apply for a position,* the applicant must fill out the form.

Prepositional phrases can also serve as an adjective or adverb. A prepositional phrase dangles when it does not, both logically and grammatically, refer to the subject.

Dangling: *With much effort,* the *report* was completed on time.
Improved: *With much effort, we* completed the report on time.

Dependent clauses also can serve as adverbs or adjectives. Sometimes part of the clause is left out although the meaning is clearly understood. Incomplete clauses are known as elliptical clauses.

The artwork [*that*] he collected was donated to the museum.

When [*he was*] interviewed, he claimed to have a master's degree.

Elliptical clauses can also dangle.

> Dangling: *While making his tour of the office,* a few changes in procedure were recommended.
> Improved: *While making his tour of the office,* he recommended a few changes in procedure.
> Improved: *While he was making his tour of the office,* a few changes in procedure were recommended.

Relative Pronouns Introducing Clauses

Be careful to select the proper relative pronoun to introduce the adjective clause. *Who* refers to persons; *which* refers to things; *what* (*that, which*) refers to things; *that* usually refers to things, but is sometimes used to refer to persons.

> The secretary *who typed this letter* has extensive experience.

> The monthly statement, *which is due Tuesday,* will contain the data.

> The report *that you have been submitting weekly* will now be required only monthly.

Placement of Modifiers

A modifier should be placed as closely as possible to the word that it modifies. This is true whether the modifier is a single word, a phrase, or a clause. Many ambiguous, and unintentionally funny, sentences result from misplaced modifiers.

> Not: I looked at the lake that I had swum *while sitting in a canoe.*
> But: *While sitting in a canoe,* I looked at the lake that I had swum.

Wherever possible, avoid placing the modifier between subject and verb and between verb and object.

> Not: The accountant, *to explain the new tax law,* used several illustrations.
> But: The accountant used several illustrations *to explain the new tax law.*

Some adverbs—*only, almost, nearly, also, quite, merely, actually*—are frequent troublemakers. The placement of the modifier changes the meaning of the sentence.

The brakes *almost* failed on every delivery. (not quite)

The brakes failed on *almost* every delivery. (very often)

Only the chairman can define the problem. (just he)

The chairman can *only* define the problem. (just define)

Do not use *hardly, only, scarcely,* and *barely* together with a negative construction. If you do, then you will have a negative construction.

Not: They *haven't only* a single blanket.
But: They *have only* a single blanket.

Not: The salesman *hasn't scarcely* sold a car.
But: The salesman *has scarcely* sold a car.

Phrases and clauses, like single-word modifiers, should be placed as closely as possible to the words that they modify.

Not: Jean looked at the report that Miguel had written *on computer sales*.
But: Jean looked at the report *on computer sales* that Miguel had written.

Not: Mr. Ismail has resigned from the presidency of the club after having served four years *to the regret of all the members*.
But: *To the regret of all the members,* Mr. Ismail has resigned from the presidency of the club.

Relative clauses should also be placed immediately after the word that they modify.

Not: The man has an appointment *who is waiting in my office*.
But: The man *who is waiting in my office* has an appointment.

Squinting Constructions

Avoid squinting constructions—that is, modifiers that are so placed that one cannot tell whether they are modifying the words immediately preceding or immediately following them.

> Squinting: The lawyer agreed *after the papers were signed* to take the case.
>
> Improved: The lawyer agreed to take the case *after the papers were signed.*
>
> Improved: *After the papers were signed,* the lawyer agreed to take the case.

Chapter 14

Basic Punctuation

The purpose of punctuation is to clarify the meaning of written language. In general, punctuation marks should prevent misreading by bringing out more clearly the author's intended meaning.

Apostrophe (')

1. Apostrophes indicate possession:

   Loretta's computer   today's temperature

2. Plural words ending in -*s* and singular words of more than one syllable ending with -*es* use only an apostrophe to show possession:

   The Arab's history   officers' quarters
   Los Angeles' pollution   Frances' desk

3. Apostrophes indicate contractions:

   don't (do not)   can't (cannot)
   I'm (I am)   aren't (are not)

Brackets [ ]

1. Brackets are used to enclose parenthetical material within a parenthesis:

   (The result [see fig. 2] is most surprising.)

2. Brackets are used to enclose interpolations that are not specifically a part of the original material being transcribed or quoted. An interpolation in brackets is usually a correction, an explanation, or a warning that the material quoted is in error:

"The bill had *not* been paid." [Emphasis added.]

"July 3 [sic] is a national holiday."

Capitalization

1. Civic organizations and governmental bodies frequently are capitalized:
   CETA, UCLA, NAACP, NCAA, FBI.

2. Complete quotations begin with a capital letter:
   Harold Levine stated, "All purchase orders must be authorized."

3. The first part of a split quotation begins with a capital letter, but the second part starts with a lower-case letter:
   "I supported a higher dividend at first," the comptroller stated, "but now I cannot justify it."

Colon (:)

1. A colon is used at the end of a complete sentence to indicate a list follows:
   We need to order new office supplies: stationery, envelopes, and business forms.
   A fundraising campaign would accomplish the following objectives: raise faculty salaries, provide student scholarships, and improve facilities.

2. A colon is not used when the list follows and incomplete statement. Do *not* use a colon in the following situations:
   We need to order stationery, envelopes, and business forms.
   A fundraising campaign would raise faculty salaries, provide student scholarships, and improve facilities.

3. Use a colon after the salutation of a business letter:
   Dear Board Member:

Comma (,)

1. Commas separate three or more items in a series:
   We need to raise productivity, improve quality, and expand marketing.

2. Commas separate independent clauses joined by conjunctions:

   Imperial Oil stock has risen sharply, but Pepco has remained flat.

   Gloria Peebles is taking maternity leave, and Stanley Markowitz will handle her accounts until she returns.

3. When a sentence begins with a dependent clause, place a comma at the end:

   After I consult the architect, I will call a board meeting.

4. Place commas around *yes* and *no*:

   Yes, the company will transfer its headquarters.

   As for the layoffs, no, we will not decrease staff.

5. Words that interrupt the flow of a sentence are set off by commas:

   I agree, however, that budgetary pressures will continue.

   As you will agree, I think, our sales prospects are not all bleak.

   The southwest, for instance, is a region that is expected to grow.

6. Use commas to set off clauses or phrases that are not essential to the meaning of the sentence:

   The foreman, complaining of assembly-line delays, has requested a meeting with management.

   Infonet, which is headquartered in Rapid City, has made a bid to acquire Cableworks.

7. Commas separate each item in as address or date:

   Route 3, Box 439, Hillsborough, North Carolina

8. A comma follows an introductory word or phrase:

   Basically, I am satisfied with my job.

   In any case, the prosecutor has ordered an end to the investigation.

9. The complimentary close of a letter is ordinarily followed by a comma, though this use is optional:

   Cordially yours,

Dash (—)

1. Long comments that interrupt the flow of the sentence may be set off by dashes, especially if the comment is a sentence itself:

   No matter how far sales decline—and I know you want to lower prices—I think that we should proceed as planned.

2. Use dashes before and after a phrase or clause that has been set off by commas and has internal punctuation of its own:

   The most popular specials—tuna melt, beef stew, and clam chowder—should be on the menu daily.

   All our warranties—which, I should remind you, are legal obligations—must be honored at all costs.

3. A dash can emphasize an afterthought, clarification, or qualification:

   The company should expand now—or pay later.

   We have only one option—sell.

4. A list of terms may be set off by a dash rather than a colon:

   Each faculty member has specific responsibilities—teaching, research, and administration.

Note: The dashes in the examples above are typeset dashes called "em" dashes; a typewriter or word processor equivalent may be formed by typing two hyphens with no space between the word and the hyphen.

Ellipses (...)

1. Use an ellipsis—three periods—to show that words are omitted from a quotation:

   The consultant reported that "company prospects look bright...if you take steps to cut costs now."

2. When an ellipsis concludes a sentence, add a fourth period:

   He started to name the states that have enacted antismog legislation: Virginia, New York, California, Florida, Maine....

Exclamation Point (!)

To emphasize a dramatic statement or a strongly held view, end with an exclamation point:

> Act now!
> We beat the deadline!
> Buy now or pay more later!

Hyphen (-)

There is no space on either side of a hyphen unless it is used at the end of a line.

1. Use a hyphen to divide a word at the end of a line.
2. Use a hyphen to connect the elements of some compounds:
   right-of-way
   south-southeast
   law-abiding citizen
   long-term loan

2. Use a hyphen to separate the letters of a spelled word:
   In front of the children, she asked me if I had brought the c-a-n-d-y.

Parentheses ( )

1. Use parentheses to set off matter that is not intended to be part of the main statement or that is not a grammatical element of the sentence, yet important enough to be included:
   This case (124 U.S. 329) is not relevant.
   The result (See fig. 2) is most surprising.
   The Portland (Oregon) Chamber of Commerce

2. A reference in parentheses a the end of a sentence is placed before the period, unless it is a complete sentence in itself:
   The specimens show great variation. (See pl. 6.)
   The specimens show great variation (pl. 6).

3. Use parentheses to enclose a figure following a spelled-out number in a legal document:

The tenant shall vacate within thirty (30) days.

4. Use parentheses to enclose numbers or letters designating items in a series:

The order of delivery will be: (a) food, (b) medicines, and (c) clothing.

Period (.)

1. A period marks the end of a statement that is a complete sentence:

The American automobile industry reported record sales.

After the chairman resigned, the board expanded its membership.

2. A period marks the end of an indirect question:

The director wondered if the staff would accept the new policy.

3. A period follows an abbreviation:

Mr.   Mrs.   Ms.

Jan.   Feb.   Mon.

etc.   tbsp.   yd.

Co.   Inc.   Ltd.

4. If an abbreviation represents more than one word, a period follows each initial:

M.D.   U.S.A.   Ph.D.

5. Official Postal Service codes do not include periods:

NY   CA   SD

Some organizations do not use periods when their titles are abbreviated:

FCC   FDA   AARP

6. When an abbreviation ends a sentence, use one period:

He moved to Boston from Charleston, S.C.

Question Mark (?)

Use a question mark at the end of a direct question:

> When can we meet to discuss this issue?

> Where are the travel vouchers?

Quotation Marks (" ") (' ')

1. Quotation marks precede and follow direct quotations:

   Staff director Francis Chu asked, "Can exceptions be made to company policy and sick leave?"

   "Extremely low" interest rates should continue to bring "record high" earnings for the bank, according to the report.

2. Quotation marks are usually placed outside other punctuation marks, with the exception of semicolons:

   The new advertising campaign has been called "negative," but I prefer to call it "aggressive."

   He said that the firm would replace "all defective parts"; labor costs are not included.

3. Quotation marks are not used at the end of an indirect quotation:

   They asked when delivery could be expected.

4. Quotation marks set off titles of short works:

   "Management Today" is the best feature in *Business Trade* magazine.

5. Single quotation marks indicate a quote within a quote:

   Frank Balducci said of the merger talks that he "opposed the process at the start but 'all's well that ends well.'"

Semicolon (;)

1. A semicolon may be used to join two independent clauses in place of a conjunction (or, and, but):

   Sales figures rose; profit margins declined.

   The staff was exhausted; the meeting was adjourned.

2. Long items in a series can be separated by semicolons:

   First the supervisor resigned, and the manager applied for her position; then the assistant manager requested a transfer; finally, the sales staff requested a meeting with senior management.

3. Items in a series with internal commas are separated with semicolons for clarity:

   The parcels were shipped to Rutherford, New Jersey; Dix Hills, New York; and Del Mar, California.

Glossary of Basic Business Terms

A

account, (1) a ledger that shows a record of debits and credits; (2) a person or company to whom credit is extended or with whom business is done

amortization, (1) reduction of debt by making gradual payments on interest and capital; (2) reduction of the value of assets by extending the depreciation over a fixed period

annuity, periodical income from life insurance, retirement system, or investment that the person receives after years of contribution to the plan

antitrust law, legislation designed to increase competition by eliminating monopolies that restrain trade

appraisal, an evaluation of the worth of goods, assets, or property

appraise, to evaluate the worth of goods, assets, or property for taxes, sale, insurance, etc.

arbitrage, the immediate purchase of a security on one market and resale of the security or its equivalent on another market, earning a quick profit from the price discrepancy

arbitration, a procedure for settling disputes in which an impartial third party, the arbitrator, makes a decision binding on the disputing parties

arrears, money, interest, or dividends that are not paid when due; an account, a person, or a company is said to be *in arrears*

assets, any property that is owned and has monetary value

B

balance, (1) calculating the difference between credits and debits of an account; (2) payment of an amount due; (3) the amount of credit in an account; (4) to equalize numbers, materials, weights, etc.

balanced budget, a budget without a surplus or a deficit where expenditures equal revenues

balance of payments, a record of statistics that indicates economic transactions between countries over a fixed period

balance of trade, the difference between the value of a country's imported merchandise and exported merchandise

balance sheet, a statement that lists assets and liabilities of an organization at a given time

barter, the exchange of goods or services without money

bear, (1) a trader who sells short, making a profit when the market declines; (2) a business pessimist

bear market, a market with falling prices

bill of lading, a document issued to a shipper by a carrier that acknowledges receipt of goods, itemizes them, and specifies terms, place, and time of delivery

bill of sale, a receipt signed by the owner that specifies the legal transfer of property to the buyer

bond, (1) a note certifying that a business or government will pay the holder a certain sum with stated interest on a particular date; (2) the legal obligation of one party to guarantee payment or performance by a second party; (3) the value of a corporation based on its total assets less its debts

book value, (1) the value of a company's assets as recorded on the financial books of the company, in contrast to intrinsic or market value; (2) the value of a corporation based on its total assets less its debts

bourse, the French term for a stock exchange, often used abroad

broker, an agent who buys or sells bond, stocks, or commodities for others on commission

bull, (1) a trader who tries to profit by rising prices; (2) a business optimist

bulletin board, a subscription computer service that displays news, messages, and information and provides access to other subscribers

bull market, market with rising prices

buy back, a company's repurchase of controlling interest of its stock at open market prices

buyer, a representative of a retail company who selects and purchases merchandise for a store

buyer's market, a market situation with abundant supply where purchasers can dictate price or terms of sale

buy on margin, to buy securities using credit from the broker as partial payment

buyout, the purchase of controlling shares of a company by employees or an outside company

C

calendar year, the twelve months from January 1 to December 31

call, (1) an option to buy a specific number of shares at a stated price within a certain time limit; (2) to demand payment; (3) to give notice that securities will be redeemed on a specific date

capital, (1) the total assets of a company; (2) money invested by owners to finance production; (3) money available for investment

capital gain, profit earned through the sale of securities, real estate, etc.

capital loss, moneys lost through the sale of securities, real estate, etc.

carrier, a business organization that transports people or merchandise

carrying charge, an additional fee paid by a customer to cover the cost of interest, service, credit, etc.

cartel, an association of producers or dealers who agree to control prices, limit production, divide territory, etc.

certificate of deposit (CD), a bank document indicating that the holder has made a time deposit, the sum of which will be left in the bank for a specific period

charter, (1) a document from a legislature or government body that confers rights and obligations on a bank or corporation; (2) the articles of a corporation; (3) to lease or hire for temporary use

chattel, (1) personal property; any property other than real estate; (2) property that is movable

clearing house, an association of banks and brokers which settles claims among its members

close corporation, a corporation controlled by a few stockholders with little or no public sale of shares

closed shop, a business that hires only union workers

closing price, the amount of the last sale of a security on one market day

collateral, property, cash, or redeemable security that a creditor offers to guarantee repayment of a loan

commerce, buying, trading, or selling goods and services

commission, the fee charged by an agent or broker for a sale, usually based on a percentage of price

commodity, (1) any goods that are physical and capable of being transported; (2) a product of trade, usually an agricultural product or a raw material, that is negotiated on a commodity exchange

common carrier, an organization that transports people or merchandise at government-regulated fixed rates

common stock, a security that indicates a share of ownership in a corporation with a claim on dividends and assets after settlement of claims by holders of preferred stock

competition, a market where a seller engages in a rivalry for profits and share of sales with other sellers

compound interest, interest that is paid on both original principal and the accrued unpaid interest

consignment, a type of sale in which the owner of a property authorizes an agent to sell the property for a fee or commission

consolidation, the union of two or more organizations into a single firm

consumer price index, a monthly governmental survey of retail prices based on a national sample

contract, an agreement between two or more parties that carries a legal obligation to perform according to certain terms

convertible, (1) bonds that can be exchanged for stock by the owner or the issuing company; (2) currency that can be exchanged for silver or gold or for the currency of a foreign country

corporation, a group of stockholders who form an association that is regarded legally as a single person

cosigner, a person who agrees to sign a note with another party and thus assumes obligations if the other party defaults

cover, the purchase of a security as compensation when selling short

credit, the ability to receive money, goods, or services against the promise of later payment

credit rating, an evaluation of a person or company based on net worth and history of meeting obligations

cut back, to halt or reduce production

D

debenture (bond), a bond backed by a company's general credit or good faith, not by specific property

deed, a legal document that conveys ownership of real estate

demand deposit, a bank deposit that can be withdrawn at any time

depreciate, to spread proportionally the cost of an asset over the time of its use

depreciation, the decline in value of property over time through use and age

discount, (1) an advanced deduction from a price by a wholesaler or retailer to someone who pays cash, pays early, or buys in quantity; (2) the amount that the face value of a security exceeds its market value; (3) interest on a loan that is collected in advance by deducting it from the amount of the loan

discount rate, (1) the minimum rate of lending; (2) the rate that the Federal Reserve Bank charges to member banks for loans

dividend, (1) corporate profits distributed to shareholders according to the size of their holdings; (2) moneys paid by certain savings associations as a type of interest or by insurance companies as a refund for overpayment

download, to copy data on a disk, an e-mail, or another information source from one computer to another computer

draft, a written order, such as a check, by which the writer authorizes a second party to make payment to a third party at the writer's expense

E

e-mail, a file or electronic message transmitted on a computer network from one person to another person

endorsement, indorsement, (1) a signature on a document; (2) the signature on the back of a title or check that guarantees the transfer of property; (3) alterations in the original terms of an insurance policy

entrepreneur, a person who takes the risk to start, manage, and own a business

equity, (1) the net worth of a firm, the amount that assets exceed liabilities; (2) the body of laws, supplementary to legal statutes, that apply to injustice and unfair practices

escape clause, a stipulation in a contract that permits a party to avoid certain undesirable consequences

escrow, a deed, contract, or other valuable document that is deposited with a third-party pending performance of some specific action

exchange, (1) to trade services or products; (2) the place where traders buy and sell commodities or securities

exchange rate, the price at which the currency of one country can buy the currency of another

excise tax, a tax that a government levies on products (usually luxury goods) produced or distributed within its territory

expense, (1) a cost to a business to operate or produce a good or service; (2) the general operating costs over an accounting period

F

fax, transmitting the facsimile of a document electronically over a telephone line from one user to another

fee, (1) payment for a service; (2) title of ownership of real estate

fiduciary, (1) a trustee of an estate or organization; (2) a transaction conducted on the basis of good faith without collateral

fiscal year, the twelve-month accounting period

fixed charges, expenses such as rent, interest, and taxes that must be paid periodically regardless of business income

float, (1) in banking, the value of checks between the writing and collecting; (2) stock that is held for speculation rather than investment and is frequently traded; (3) an unfunded debt or unsold part of an offering of securities

foreclosure, a legal proceeding that requires the sale or forfeiture of a mortgaged property when the mortgagor is unable to pay the debt

franchise, a right granted by a government to a person or firm to conduct a specific business at a stated place and time

free and clear, titles (usually of real estate) with no lien or mortgage

frozen assets, securities, properties, or moneys of a business that cannot be sold quickly without great loss

funded debt, debt in the form of a bond or other long-term note

fungible goods, products that come in standard units, such as grain or coffee, which can be negotiated one for the other

futures, contracts for securities or commodities that are bought and sold for later delivery

G

gold standard, use of gold to back the value of monetary units, such as the system prevailing in the United States before 1934

goodwill, the intangible assets of a business based on reputation, consumer relations, quality of service, etc.

greenmail, the legal practice of buying stock in a company under the threat of a hostile takeover, forcing the company's management to purchase stock (inflating its price) to retain control

gross income, total gains or receipts before deductions

gross profit, total receipts beyond the cost of goods sold without deducting for expenses

H

hardware, the components of a computer including processor, monitor, terminals, drives, printer, etc.

hedging, buying and selling to reduce the risk of loss

holding company, a corporation that owns enough shares in other firms to control them

hostile takeover, a predatory bid or merger proposal that is contrary to the wishes of the company's management

I

indemnity, (1) an agreement that protects against damage or loss; (2) the compensation granted for the loss, up to the insurance policy's face value

indenture, (1) a written agreement that establishes the conditions of a bond issue and authorizes an independent trustee to act on behalf of the bondholders; (2) a deed including several parties; (3) a contract that binds the labor of a person to an employer for a stated period

individual retirement account (IRA), a plan whereby a person can put a percentage of income into a fund that is exempt from tax as income or earnings until the person's retirement

interface, (1) the connection or coordination between two or more systems; (2) the boundary between parts or systems

internet, an electronic system that, through telephone lines and satellite links, connects computers to networks such as e-mail and the World Wide Web

inventory, (1) a list of all items owned by a person or firm and their value; (2) raw material, products in process, and finished goods scheduled for use or for sale

J-K

job description, a listing of the qualifications and obligations for a specific position

job shop, a producer who makes custom orders rather than items for general inventory

junk bond, a high-risk, high-interest bearing bond issued by a company that is attempting to raise capital quickly

L

letter of credit, a letter from a bank that requests other institutions to extend credit or advance money to the holder and guarantees reimbursement

leverage, financial speculation using borrowed capital with the expectation that future profits will be greater than interest payments

liability, (1) debt owed; (2) an obligation by a person or company that is subject to a claim

license, a permit granted by a government, person, or institution to do certain acts or to conduct a specific business

lien, a legal right claimed by a creditor against the property of a debtor

limited, (1) a corporation where shareholders' liability is confined to the amount of their investment; (2) a corporation, chiefly in British usage

limited partnership, ownership in a business by investment only, with no role in management and with liability restricted to the size of investment

line of credit, the maximum amount that a lending institution will lend to a borrower

liquid assets, assets that are cash or that can be readily converted to cash

liquidation, (1) converting assets to cash either to take a profit or terminate a business; (2) fulfillment of an obligation, such as repaying a loan

listserv, a service that provides free e-mail to users on a subject of particular interest

loss leader, merchandise sold below cost to attract customers

M

margin, (1) the difference between the price paid and the price sold; (2) to buy a security with a loan from a broker as partial payment

market price, (1) the prevailing price of an item at the time; (2) the price established by supply and demand; (3) the last price quoted for a security when traded

merger, the uniting of two or more businesses under the ownership of the firm that acquires the stock of the other business(es)

money market, the system through which transactions are made in short-term funds such as loans, gold, securities, or foreign currencies

money market fund, a mutual fund that deals with short-term securities

moratorium, a period, granted legally, in which a debtor is permitted to delay payment of an obligation beyond the date due

mortgage, a legal arrangement that places title in real estate or property as security for payment of a loan

multinational company, a company that operates in a global market with management centers, production facilities, and assets in several countries

municipal bond, a bond issued by a local government

mutual company, a corporation without stock whose officers are elected and whose profits are shared by policyholders or members according to their amount of business, as with mutual insurance companies or mutual savings banks

mutual fund, an open-end investment trust that issues shares by customer demand and gives management broad power to select investments

N

negotiable, documents that can be transferred from one person to another through endorsement or other legal strictures

net assets, working capital, the amount that remains after deductions for liabilities

O

odd lot, in commodity and security sales, an amount that differs from the customary trading unit, i.e., less than 100 shares of stock

offer, contract terms proposed by one party (offeror) to another party (offeree)

open shop, a business that employs union and nonunion workers on equal terms

opening price, the amount of the first sale of a security on a market day

option, (1) a legally binding promise to keep an offer open for a specific period; (2) a right to buy or sell a property within a specific period; (3) alternatives available after discontinuing payment of insurance premiums

overdraft, the amount that a demand for payment, such as a check, exceeds the balance of funds on deposit

over-the-counter, securities transactions that occur outside regular stock exchanges, whether or not the security is listed on an exchange

P

paper profit, a profit that would be obtained if a security or property were actually sold rather than retained

parity price, a sum paid to American farmers for their produce to protect their purchasing power

partnership, a business of two or more owners who share losses and profits

patent, an exclusive right granted by a government to the inventor to manufacture, use, or sell an invention for a specific period

payback period, the estimated time required to recover the cost of a capital investment

per capita, Latin for "by head," that is, for each person

petty cash, a limited cash fund used for minor expenses

pool, (1) a combine of investors who seek to control the market price of a company's stock; (2) an agreement among companies to manipulate prices by controlling competition; (3) a group of insurers organized to share a policy risk

postdating, affixing a date to a document later than it was signed

posting, transferring entries form a journal to a ledger in accounting

power of attorney, a document that authorizes an agent to act one one's behalf

predating, affixing a date to a document earlier than it was signed

preferred stock, stock entitling the holder to receive dividends and assets upon liquidation before the holders of common stock

premium, (1) the sum a policyholder pays for an insurance policy; (2) a bonus or special payment in goods, services, or cash; (3) the difference between the price of a stock or bond and its face value

price, the amount of money that represents the exchange value of a service or goods

price fixing, the regulation of prices by agreement of private persons or firms, usually illegally, or legally by the government

price index, a table that indicates the relative change in the price of an item over time, expressed as a ratio

price level, the average of prevailing prices at a specific time

prime rate, the interest rate that a bank charges to its best customers for short-term loans

principal, (1) a person who is represented by an agent; (2) the sum of capital loaned or invested, distinguished from interest or profits

probate, judicial process that verifies and registers the legitimacy of a last will and testament after death

productivity, the quantity of output by one factor (e.g., a worker) over a unit of time

profit, (1) the amount that revenues exceed the costs of obtaining revenues; (2) the amount earned beyond capital investment when prices of goods sold exceed cost of production

profit margin, a ratio or percentage indicating the relation between gross profit and net sales

profit sharing, distribution of a share of a business' profits to its employees in addition to wages

progressive tax, a tax levied at increasingly higher rates as the income level or the tax base becomes higher

promissory note, a written promise to pay a specific sum to a particular person (often the bearer) on a certain date or on demand

property, goods and rights that may be owned

property tax, a tax levied on personal articles owned or on land and buildings

prorate, (1) to apportion a cost over an account according to some system of distribution; (2) to distribute the total amount of insurance over several items in proportion to their value

prospectus, a statement from a corporation containing financial details and data about an offer of securities

proxy, a written statement from a shareholder authorizing another person to represent and vote on behalf of the shareholder

public domain, (1) a publication or product that is not legally protected by patent or copyright; (2) government-owned land

pump priming, large governmental expenditures to stimulate economic growth through increased purchase power and employment

purchase order, a form that a buyer sends to a seller authorizing a sale and specifying the type, quantity, and often the price of goods

purchasing power, the value of money according to its ability to buy goods

Q

quality control, the system necessary to insure that a company's goods or services meet minimum standards

R

rate of return, (1) the rate of earned profit compared to the amount of capital invested; (2) a rate permitted by a regulatory agency to a public utility to insure fair profit on capital investment and to protect consumers

real cost, (1) the cost after compensating for changes in purchasing power; (2) the cost when compared to other uses of the same money; (3) the cost in concrete terms of measurement such as tons, square feet, labor hours, etc.

real estate, land with buildings, fences, or other immovable improvements

real property, land, buildings, and improvements in contrast to personal property

realtor, a broker of real estate

rebate, the return of a portion of a payment

receiver, an impartial person appointed by a court to administer disputed funds or property by reason of debt

receivership, a legal action entailing a court's appointment of an impartial manager to administer the funds and property of a person or firm unable to pay debts

redemption, (1) the repurchase of a note, stock, bond, or currency by the issuing agency, usually for cash; (2) after foreclosure, the freeing of the mortgage lien by payment of obligations past due

register, (1) an accounting book; (2) a list of shareholders; (3) a ship's papers

registrar, a person who signs stock certificates and ensures that the stock is authorized by the issuing company

remainder, (1) a future interest in real estate for a party other than the grantor; (2) overstocked books that publishers sell at reduced costs

rent, a payment for the use of property

repurchase agreement, selling securities on a temporary basis with the seller agreeing to buy them back after an agreed time

reserves, (1) the funds set aside from profits for the payment of debt or other need; (2) funds an insurer uses to meet claims and other liabilities

resources, assets

retail, selling goods directly to consumers for final consumption

return, profit rate relative to the value of capital invested

risk, the probability of loss or profit of an investment

right-to-work laws, legislation that forbids a closed-shop (and sometimes a union-shop) clause in labor contracts

round lot, a conventional trading unit, such as 100 shares of stock or $1000 par value for bonds

royalty, a price paid in return for a right, to an author for a book, to a land-owner to mine, to a patent holder to manufacture, etc.

rubber check, slang for a bad check

S

sale, (1) the transfer of title of ownership of property for a price; (2) the chance to buy goods at a reduced price

salvage, (1) the value of an item for other than original use or for resale; (2) in insurance, the value of property after it has sustained damage

saturation point, a market whose potential has been fully exploited

scrip, a certificate used as currency or as a share of stock

seasonal variation, a regularly recurring pattern of change in business and economics that occurs yearly due to climate, vacations, holidays, or other consistent factors

security, (1) a written instrument that indicates indebtedness or ownership, such as a bond, stock, bill, mortgage, receipt, and so on; (2) a pledge made to a lender that assures repayment of a loan

self-liquidating, a loan or investment that yields a return sufficient to pay for itself

sell short, to sell a security or commodity not actually owned in anticipation of a decline in price

seller's market, a market where demand exceeds supply, hence sellers can control prices or terms of sale

settlement, (1) resolution of a dispute outside of court; (2) completion of a financial obligation

share, a unit or portion of ownership in a business

shaving a note, (1) discounting a note at a higher than legal rate of interest or above the market price; (2) paying a charge for extra time to deliver or pay a security

silent partner, a person who invests in a partnership but does not actively participate in management

simple interest, interest paid on the principal only, not on accumulated interest

sinking fund, a sum consisting of moneys set aside regularly and usually invested at interest to pay debts, redeem bonds, meet expenses, etc.

slowdown, a deliberate reduction in the rate of production by management or, more often, by labor

solvency, (1) the ability of a business to meet its obligations when due; (2) the condition wherein a business' total assets exceed its total liabilities

specie, coins, usually of gold or silver, rather than coins of base metal or paper money

speculation, sales or purchases of goods or securities with the intent of quick profit rather than long-term investment

stock, (1) a share of ownership in a corporation; (2) the certificate itself representing the share; (3) the total sum of capital invested in the business; (4) merchandise a company holds for sale and the materials necessary for a business to finish that merchandise

stock exchange, a market where brokers buy and sell stocks and bonds during certain hours and under proscribed rules

stop order, an order to buy or sell a specified number of shares of a security when the market price reaches a certain level

stop payment, a depositor's order to a bank not to make payment on a certain stock

subcontract, an arrangement whereby a prime contractor with responsibility for a complete project awards a portion of the work to another firm

subsidy, a governmental grant to a person, firm, or industry to encourage productivity or to support an effort beneficial to the public

supply, the producer's readiness to sell a certain quantity of goods or services at a specified price, time, and market

supply-side economics, a theory claiming that the reduction of taxes will generate incentives that will expand the nation's output

surety bond, a form of insurance wherein a third party (the surety) promises to reimburse the insured party named in the bond against the default of another party (the principal)

surplus, (1) the excess of revenue over expenditure; (2) earnings from production beyond the cost of production; (3) an excess of products over market demand

surtax, an extra tax beyond the normal rate

syndicate, a group of persons or corporations organized to act with a common purpose, especially in the sale of securities

T

tangible assets, (1) resources that are substantial, such as real estate; (2) resources including stock, property, or cash as opposed to such intangible assets as goodwill, rights, or patents

tariff, (1) a customs tax on goods as they enter or (less often) leave a country; (2) a schedule of rates, changes or rules, usually of transportation

tender, (1) an offer to pay money, perform a service, or deliver goods; (2) a means to acquire control of a corporation by asking shareholders to sell their stock at a fixed price by a certain date

time deposit, a bank deposit that cannot be withdrawn before a specified time or without advanced notice

title, a document that gives evidence of ownership

trading down, buying and selling lower-priced merchandise to increase profits through higher sales volume

trading up, buying and selling higher-priced merchandise to increase the profit margin

transfer agent, a person who records transactions of a company's stock and is responsible for issuing shares and keeping records of shareholders

trust, (1) a legal procedure in which one party (the trustee) holds title to a property for the benefit of another party (the beneficiary); (2) an association or corporation with a single board of trustees that exercises a monopoly on the production and distribution of a good or service

turnover, (1) the number of times a cycle repeats itself in a given period; (2) the number of workers hired to replace those who leave relative to the total number of workers; (3) sale of goods

U-Z

underwriter, a person or organization that guarantees a risk against losses, especially in insurance and investment of stocks

unlisted security, a security traded over the counter and not negotiated on a recognized stock exchange

venture capital, a risky or speculative investment for the forming of new businesses, particularly small ones

voucher, a document that acknowledges the receipt of a payment

warrant, (1) a legal document authorizing arrest; (2) a certificate granting an option to purchase stock at a specified price within a stated period

warranty, a guarantee that certain facts are true as represented

web site, a computer file that is accessible through the World Wide Web

wholesale, buying and selling by a middleman to retailers or to major commercial users, but rarely to the ultimate consumers

World Wide Web, a global electronic network that allows users to connect to Web sites, data banks, and other information sources through the Internet

write-off, an accounting procedure to compensate for bad debts or losses by balancing them against earnings or other funds

yield, (1) rate of return as a percentage; (2) the ratio between the dividend of a stock and its purchase price

Notes

Notes

Notes

Notes

Notes

Notes

Notes

Notes

Notes

Notes

Notes

Notes

Notes

Notes

Notes

Notes

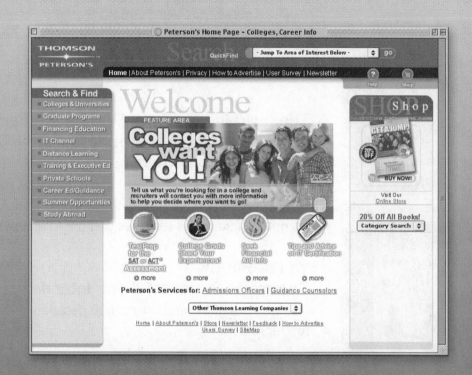